Editor

Dona Herweck Rice

Illustrator

Keith Vasconcelles

Cover Artist

Blanca Apodaca La Bounty

Editor-in-Chief

Sharon Coan, M.S. Ed.

Art Manager

Elayne Roberts

Imaging

Alfred Lau

Product Manager

Phil Garcia

Publisher

Mary D. Smith, M.S. Ed.

Celebrate
CHRISTMAS
Around The World

Author

Beth Dvergsten Stevens

Teacher Created Resources, Inc.

6421 Industry Way

Westminster, CA 92683

www.teachercreated.com

©1994 Teacher Created Resources, Inc.

Reprinted, 2006

Made in U.S.A.

ISBN-1-55734-485-X

Table of Contents

Introduction

WHAT IS CHRISTMAS?

Christmas is the most celebrated holiday in the world. Individuals on every continent celebrate it, and more than one hundred countries officially recognize it in one way or another. Although Christmas has a Christian origin, many of today's traditions include secular practices. Yet, whether it is viewed as a holiday or a holy day, Christmas has become a bustling, hopeful, happy time of year for people throughout the world.

Every country's Christmas celebrations vary according to that country's climate, beliefs, folklore, and traditions. However, many Christmas practices and symbols are common to a number of countries. Most countries set up nativity scenes to recall Jesus' humble birth. Bells ring out the good news everywhere. Stars and candles represent the light and joy of Christmas. Angels, shepherds, and Wise Men are an important part of many Christmas gatherings. To the joy of children everywhere, gift giving is a common practice, though the giver may not be the same from one country to the next.

In some countries, gifts are delivered by young girls dressed in white. In others, the gift giver is some variation of a man dressed in red. Gifts may be left in shoes, stockings, or cradles, but the secretive nature is universal. Often a nasty character accompanies the gift giver, and those children who have been naughty receive coal, straw, or other unpleasant gifts from this person.

Another universal practice is the decoration of houses with greenery such as evergreen trees, holly, ivy, and mistletoe. (Evergreen plants were once thought to contain magical powers because they remained green throughout the winter months.) Ornaments and other decorations are common to all countries, but the symbols and materials used are special to each one. But no matter which country's traditions are in practice, the spirit of the season tends to remain the same. The expression of joy and hope is constant, as is the desire to share and give to others from one's own plenty. People around the world reach out to renew friendships and family relationships, and the feelings of goodwill, peacemaking, generosity, and kindness abound. All these expressions manifest themselves in traditional celebrations. While recognizing the variety of customs around the world, it is also important to recognize the commonalities shared. Christmas truly is a universal celebration.

THE HISTORY OF CHRISTMAS

Christmas is a religious celebration which honors the birth of Jesus Christ two thousand years ago in the tiny country now called Israel. The story is found in the Bible. People who believe that Jesus was the son of God are called Christians. They believe Christ was born to teach and save his people, so Christians find great joy and happiness in this holiday. It is a celebration of life and light, and their festivities reflect these feelings.

Introduction *(cont.)*

THE HISTORY OF CHRISTMAS *(cont.)*

Although the exact date of Jesus' birth is unclear, December 25 is the date proclaimed as Christ's birthday, and December 24 is called Christmas Eve. There is a good reason why the early Christians chose December 25 to recognize the holy day. Hundreds of years before Christ's birth, people in different parts of the world had established year-end festivals. In northern Europe, for example, people worshipped the sun. They knew the sun brought heat and light so crops could grow and life could continue. However, they did not understand astronomy or the change of seasons. They only knew that during this time of year, there was less sunlight and the days got progressively shorter. They feared the sun god was punishing them and the sun might disappear forever. If this happened, all living things would die. So, they danced to call the sun and lit great fires with huge logs (Yule logs) to help the sun god make light again.

Science shows us that the short days are caused by the tilt of the earth as it travels around the sun. As the fall months pass, less sunlight reaches the northern hemisphere until about December 22, the shortest day of the year and the official first day of winter. For the next few days, the sun seems to stand still. This is called the winter solstice. Then, the days slowly begin to lengthen again and there is more light. At this point, the people of long ago thought their fires had appeased the sun god, and they feasted and rejoiced to celebrate the sun's return.

The Roman people also celebrated near the year's end with a festival called *Saturnalia.* This was to honor the god of agriculture after a successful harvest. They brought evergreen branches into their homes because they believed they had magical powers. They celebrated wildly with feasting, dancing, games, masks, parades, and the exchange of gifts.

In December, the ancient Hebrews celebrated the Feast of Lights or *Hanukkah.* It, too, included gift giving, games, and good food. Hanukkah, of course, is still a widely celebrated holiday.

The early Christians wanted to convert all *pagans* (non-Christians) to their religion, but they faced an uphill battle. The pagans enjoyed their festivities and did not want to give them up. To persuade the pagans to become Christians, religious leaders combined their holy day with the festivities already in place, thereby allowing the people to continue practicing some of their customs. Not surprisingly, the Christians began enjoying them, too. This is the reason why many of the ancient customs, such as Yule logs, Christmas trees, and gift exchanges, have become part of modern Christmas celebrations.

THE CHRISTMAS SEASON

The Christmas season starts at different times in various countries. Advent is the beginning of the religious season as believers prepare for the "coming" of the Christ child. Advent begins on the fourth Sunday before Christmas and is often marked by an Advent wreath and five candles anticipating Christ's birth.

In some places, festivities begin on December 6, which is called St. Nicholas Day. In other places, the celebration begins with the first star sighted on Christmas Eve. Celebrations and festivities may last until January 1, which is New Year's Day, or continue for twelve days until January 6, which is called Three Kings' Day or The Feast of the Epiphany. (Hence, we have "the twelve days of Christmas.")

Epiphany is for many people a major holiday. It commemorates the arrival of the Three Wise Men (or Three Kings) in Bethlehem. Often, gifts are given just as the Wise Men gave gifts to the Christ child long ago. However, some countries tell of a female gift giver (Befana or Baboushka) who delivers gifts on January 6. The stories of these ladies are found in this book in the sections on Italy and Russia.

Introduction *(cont.)*

THE BIRTH OF JESUS

In the Bible, the story of Jesus' birth is found in *Matthew 1:18–2:23* and *Luke 2:1–21*. You might wish to share those stories with the children, or the following version can be read aloud.

Ever since creation, people have made mistakes and failed to do all the things God commanded of them. But long ago, God promised his people that someday he would send someone special to make up for their sins. This someone special would be called a *savior* and a *king* because he would save the people from their errors and rule them justly. The people waited a long time. It was sometimes very difficult because their Roman ruler was cruel and unfair.

The people were not sure exactly how this savior would arrive. God chose a poor and humble young woman named Mary to be the mother. He sent an angel named Gabriel to tell Mary that she would have a special baby and she was to name him "Jesus." This child would be the savior of the world, and God would be the heavenly father. Now Mary was very surprised at this news, but she was faithful to God and happily accepted it. After some difficulty, Joseph, the man to whom Mary was engaged, also accepted the news and promised to be Jesus' earthly father.

Time passed, and soon Mary's baby was to be born. But at this same time, the Roman emperor decided to force the people of Judea to travel to their families' hometowns and be counted in a census. (He wanted to be sure he had everyone's name so he could collect taxes from them all.) This was difficult for Mary and Joseph, but they traveled all the way from Nazareth to the little town of Bethlehem. (Joseph was from the family of David, and this was David's hometown.) They were very tired, but the town was so crowded with other travelers that they could not find a single place to rest. Finally, they stopped at a stable. It was used to keep horses, cows, and other animals at night, so it was not very comfortable. But during that night, Mary's baby was born. She wrapped him lovingly in cloths and laid him in a hay-filled manger, which became his bed. (A manger is actually a food box from which animals eat.) Here was the long-awaited savior, born in a barn and sleeping in a manger, and no one even knew about it except Mary, Joseph, and the animals.

But, of course, God knew, too. He sent an angel to earth to tell the news to some shepherds who were tending their flocks of sheep near Bethlehem. The angel said, "Behold, I bring you tidings of great joy which shall be to all the people; for there is born this day in the city of David, a Savior which is Christ the Lord." The angel told the shepherds where to find the baby, and then more angels filled the sky with great singing. The shepherds were frightened at first, but then they felt amazed at this message and hurried immediately to Bethlehem to find the child. They found him just as the angel said, and they bowed down before the baby when they realized this was the promised one from God. When the shepherds left, they were filled with happiness and told everyone they met about the things they had seen and heard.

At about this same time in a land far to the east, there lived some men who studied the stars. One night, they noticed a new star in the sky, and they somehow knew it would lead them to a new king. They knew they must follow it. They gathered precious gifts and traveled on camels by night when the star was visible. As they got close to Jerusalem, they asked people about the new king. No one seemed to know much. The wicked ruler, Herod, heard there were three men looking for a new king. This worried Herod because he did not want a new king to take his place. So, he called the three strangers to his palace and lied to them. He said that he wanted to honor the new king, too. He told them to report back to him as soon as they found this king.

Introduction *(cont.)*

THE BIRTH OF JESUS *(cont.)*

The Three Wise Men found the bright star again and it led them to the stable in Bethlehem where the baby lay. They kneeled before Jesus and offered their precious gifts of gold, frankincense, and myrrh. Before returning to their own home, they were warned in a dream *not* to tell Herod. They went home by another road instead.

Herod was angry. He wanted to kill this new king. But God protected Jesus. God sent Joseph a dream that told him to take Mary and Jesus to Egypt until it was safe to return. Quickly, Joseph and Mary gathered up Jesus and their belongings and began the long journey to safety.

SAINT NICHOLAS

Gift giving is a universal Christmas practice, but it is done differently in each country. Most countries tell of a character who secretly delivers gifts to good children during the night. The gift giver who started this practice was a man called Nicholas. He lived in what is now Turkey. He was a kind and generous Christian, and when his wealthy parents died, he spent his life secretly doing good things for children and performing miracles. There are many stories telling of his aid to sailors, merchants, and children, but the most famous one is the story of a poor man's three daughters.

These three daughters needed dowries before they could marry. (This was a common practice in those days. Parents needed to provide some money, land, or other material possessions to prove their daughter's worth for marriage.) But, of course, the poor man had no money. Nicholas knew this, and when the oldest daughter was ready to marry, he dropped a bag of gold down the chimney (or some say through an open window) at night, and it landed in the girl's stocking, which had been hung to dry. In the morning, she found it. It seemed like a miracle. Nicholas did the same thing for the next daughter. When it came time for the last daughter to marry, the poor man stayed awake to discover who the gift giver was. When he saw it was Nicholas, he thanked him and eventually told others of his good deeds. As other stories of Nicholas' generosity spread, people started to thank him for any unexpected gift. After he died, Nicholas became the patron saint of many countries. Gift giving takes place on his feast day, December 6. This is also why children today leave stockings or shoes out to receive the secret gifts—such as oranges which represent Nicholas' gold. Since December 6 is so close to Christmas, some countries have maintained the tradition but moved its date to December 24, Christmas Eve, as a reminder of God's gift of the Christ child. In some countries, children receive gifts on both dates.

St. Nicholas is pictured in a wide variety of ways, and his name is different in each country. He is Father Christmas, Kris Kringle, Santa Claus, and more. He has become an interesting mix of religious and secular customs. But usually he is a kind person who is bearded and dressed in long robes. He carries gifts in some container and travels on or with some sort of animal. In many countries, he also has a traveling companion who may not be so kind and punishes the naughty children.

Teaching Strategies

SCHOOL AND PARENTAL PHILOSOPHY

Before beginning a unit on holidays, become acquainted with your school's philosophy on the topic. Some schools frown upon the celebration or study of holidays. This book is written from a social studies perspective as Christmas is a theme with universal ties and appeal. Activities within the book cross the curriculum for greater hands-on learning experiences.

PLANNING FOR EXCEPTIONS

Know your students. To meet the needs of those students who cannot celebrate holidays, be prepared to provide a variety of ways to accomplish your goals. Perhaps a focus on the history, art, or literature aspects of a culture would be valuable. Allow students to choose activities from acceptable alternatives whenever possible. The wide variety of activities within this book should allow flexibility for you and your students. If you offer an activity based on the religious aspect of Christmas, be prepared to offer a secular one as well. Remember, you may not actually be doing the celebrating so much as learning about how the holiday is celebrated around the world.

Students can be helped to know that not everyone celebrates Christmas, and that is all right. No one's beliefs are being questioned or threatened. No one is judging the beliefs of others. Rather, the students will be learning interesting information about other countries. Hopefully, this will replace indifference with interest and encourage further discovery and exploration.

USE YOUR RESOURCES

Teachers cannot know it all. The students' families are a great source of information. Ask them to share their heritage and culture with your class. Invite them to visit, send things to class, or share their knowledge in other ways.

Use the resources available to you. Some helpful resource books are listed in the bibliography. Most should be available at your public library. A partial list of towns in the United States with strong ethnic ties is also included (page 113). You may discover more with help from your students.

To put cultural learning in perspective, it helps to learn about the geography of each nation. A world map is included on page 10. Use current maps and globes whenever possible to show students where these countries are in comparison to your own. Look at the topography and compare the sizes of different countries. Find out which ones are "neighbors" and compare their traditions. Locate familiar cities. Help children find out where their ancestors lived. Become knowledgeable yourself so you can help your students become comfortable with the ever-changing, world.

Gathering the following resources will assist you in carrying out activities for your classroom.

- world map
- zip code book
- newspapers
- world almanac
- bird and animal identification books
- state maps or atlas
- phone books
- globe
- current encyclopedias
- calculators

ETHNIC REPRESENTATIVES

Once you have chosen those countries you wish to study, look around for some knowledgeable, ethnic representatives in your students' families. Invite these individuals to speak to your class. They may share family customs, foods, or a sense of pride that will be rich and rewarding to your students. Let parents and relatives feel they are welcome. You may create some lasting memories for everyone involved.

Teaching Strategies *(cont.)*

ETHNIC CITIES IN THE UNITED STATES

On page 113, you will find a partial listing of cities and towns in the United States with strong ethnic roots and traditions. In October or November, have your students write letters to some of these communities to gather information about the customs still followed today. Include questions about foods and recipes, typical family names, and current practices on Christmas Eve, Christmas Day, and Epiphany.

A current world almanac can give you the addresses and phone numbers for each state's tourism office. Most offices can give you more specific information on a town and the correct address for your letters. Letters can be addressed to the mayor, city manager, or Chamber of Commerce. The almanac lists the names of officials for larger cities. For smaller towns, address letters to "Mayor of (town name)."

PREPARING TO COOK

There are ethnic recipes included with many countries. Cooking experiences can be very rewarding for children as long as they are well organized. Be sure you have calculated and purchased the correct quantities of ingredients before attempting a cooking activity. Decide how much participation you want from the children. Some activities might lend themselves to demonstrations by the teacher. Others are very student directed and will require little assistance from adult supervisors.

Students must wash their hands if they will be helping mix, shape, or eat the foods. This can be handled quite easily if the activity is scheduled after a restroom break and they understand the importance of sanitation.

It might be fun to solicit help from parents when undertaking a new cooking activity. Perhaps they could make a sample ethnic food at home and bring it to school as part of a taste-testing party. Or perhaps they could assist you in the classroom. You may also wish to solicit small food donations from the students if your budget does not allow the purchase of ingredients.

All recipes in this book are formatted for easy duplication. You will notice a border of holly to indicate each one. These can be grouped together into a recipe file or booklet to be shared with families. Parents will appreciate receiving copies of the recipes their children have made (and even samples of the products, if possible). This is a good way to open communication between students and their families, and it helps everyone appreciate the lessons better.

LANGUAGE ACTIVITIES

There are many legends and stories rich in cultural heritage. Read age-appropriate ones aloud to your class and help them understand the meanings. Use the bibliography at the back of this book and check the resources in your library.

Christmas carols are also plentiful and varied. The words to many songs are included in this book. They can be duplicated easily for the students. Tunes can be found in many of the books listed in the bibliography. Students may wish to compile a songbook to take home.

Encourage writing skills by having students write letters and cards as well as their own Christmas stories, legends, and carols. Offer opportunities for both individual and group work. Some suggested activities are included in the various country sections.

Using the information gathered from your letters to cities with strong ethnic ties, have the students write stories about typical holidays in those countries represented. Use traditional names, customs, and practices to tell the story. Illustrate these and display them in your library.

8

Teaching Strategies *(cont.)*

ARTS AND CRAFTS ACTIVITIES

There are many patterns and suggestions for arts and crafts activities linked to each country. All are intended to enhance understanding about the countries studied. Ornaments and other decorations are intended to be used and displayed by the students, so encourage them to complete each one to the best of their abilities.

Patterns may be reproduced as needed for your classroom. To complete these, you will need paper, glue, and other art supplies which are normally available within a school. Some activities require additional materials. Since children of all ages learn best by hands-on activities, collecting some of the following materials will expand your choices of activities:

- old Christmas cards
- old cereal boxes, flattened with liners removed
- old newspapers
- flour (to be used in making paste or doughs)
- tin cans (variety of sizes, cleaned, and sharp edges smoothed)
- plastic drinking straws
- fabric scraps and trims such as ribbon, rickrack, etc.
- yarn or cotton thread
- plastic "Easter" eggs or those from old pantyhose
- old magazines
- pipe cleaners
- razor knife (for teacher use only)
- red (or pink) and green plastic wrap
- tissue paper
- glue gun (low temperature for safety)
- aluminum foil
- waxed paper
- poster board
- self-adhesive paper (wood grain and clear)
- sawdust (from a woodworking hobbyist, store, or classroom)
- straw (from a farm or craft store)
- thick, white craft glue
- old envelopes

TAKE-HOME STUDENT BOOKLETS

Pages 114–125 are designed for students to create a take-home booklet about each country studied. You may pick and choose which countries to include, and their booklet will reflect the information learned. Encourage your students to share the booklets with their families.

The full-page format is designed primarily for lower elementary students. They may practice writing skills by printing the country's name at the top and perhaps writing three facts or words they learned. The center portion is for illustrations or other activities as directed by the teacher.

The half-page format is designed for upper elementary students. The summary portion can be used as a review or stimulus for student-created work inside. Flow charts, webs, illustrations, or facts fit nicely inside. Students can add details to the existing illustration and personalize it as desired.

If preferred, the summary portions may be used as part of a parent information letter. Adding student illustrations will make it meaningful to parents and children.

Teaching Strategies *(cont.)*

WORLD MAP

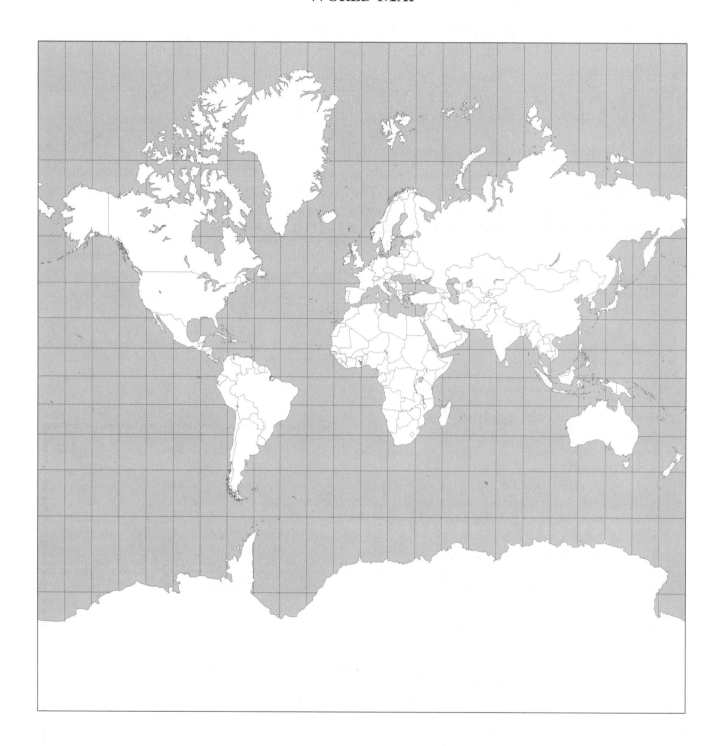

Austria

Austrians begin their Christmas celebrations on St. Nicholas Day and end them a month later on Epiphany. Many of their celebrations are like those found in Germany. (See pages 27–31.)

Evergreens decorate Austrian homes at Christmastime. Sometimes they hang the decorated tip of a fir tree upside down in the corner of their best room. This becomes "Lord God's Corner."

Christkind (the Christ child) leaves unwrapped gifts beneath the Christmas tree on Christmas Eve. When the children, who have been sleeping, see the tree for the first time, they are delighted with both the gifts and the tree, which they believe Christkind has helped to decorate. The tree may hold colorful paper ornaments, nuts, apples, and candles. There may also be roses, a special Austrian Christmas symbol.

Families often attend midnight church services on Christmas Eve, and on Christmas Day they eat a large meal of roast goose with all the trimmings. They may join together to sing Christmas carols, many of which have come from Austria. Perhaps most popular is the Austrian carol "Silent Night" (page 12), which is believed to be the most widely sung carol in the world.

ACTIVITIES

1. Ask someone who knows sign language to teach the class "Silent Night."
2. Have the students define the following words and phrases: silent, holy, 'round yon, quake, glories, heavenly hosts, radiant beams, and redeeming grace. Students might also illustrate the meaning of the song.
3. Write new words to fit the tune of "Silent Night."
4. Make marzipan. The recipe is below.

Marzipan

Marzipan is a favorite Austrian holiday candy. It is typically shaped like fruits, vegetables, flowers, or animals.

Ingredients:
- 4 oz. (120 g) almond paste (in tube or block)
- $\frac{1}{2}$ c. (125 mL) powdered sugar
- 1 T. (15 mL) light corn syrup
- 1-2 drops food coloring (or cocoa for brown)

Preparation:
1. Break up the paste with your hands in a small bowl.
2. Knead in the sugar and corn syrup, squeezing out all lumps until the paste is smooth.
3. Decide what shapes you wish to create, and add the appropriate food coloring to small quantities of the kneaded paste. Work the color in until the paste is evenly colored.
4. Make small shapes with your hands, spoons, or other utensils. If desired, press whole cloves into orange and apple shapes for stems. Think of other ways to add details to each figure.
5. Let dry slightly and display on a doily-lined platter before eating.

STILLE NACHT *(German)*

Stille Nacht, Heilige Nacht;

All' schläft, einsam wacht,

Nur das traute hoch heilige Paar.

Holder Knabe im lockigen Haar,

Schlaf in himmlischer Ruh,

Schlaf in himmlischer Ruh.

SILENT NIGHT *(English)*

Silent night, Holy night

All is calm, all is bright.

'Round yon Virgin Mother and Child

Holy Infant so tender and mild,

Sleep in heavenly peace,

Sleep in heavenly peace.

Silent night, Holy night

Shepherds quake at the sight.

Glories stream from heaven afar

Heavenly hosts sing Alleluia;

Christ the Savior is born,

Christ the Savior is born.

Silent night, Holy night

Son of God, love's pure light.

Radiant beams from Thy holy face,

With the dawn of redeeming grace,

Jesus, Lord, at Thy birth,

Jesus, Lord, at Thy birth.

Brazil

To greet you at Christmastime, the Brazilians might say, *"Boas Festas!"* (good holidays) and, *"Feliz Natal!"* (happy Christmas). In Brazil, Christmas is a warm holiday, in more ways than one. People everywhere are in happy, open spirits, and the country itself is literally very warm. Papa Noël, the gift giver, comes in through an open window since most homes have no need of a fireplace. He places the gifts in children's shoes which have been left under the Christmas tree.

Even though many people cannot afford to buy gifts or decorations for their homes, the spirit is festive and joyful. Dances, picnics, and fireworks are free and can be enjoyed by everyone. The loudest fireworks are kept until Epiphany. When they are ignited, everyone knows the Christmas season is finished.

Brazilians, many of whom are Catholics, have a tradition of helping the poor at Christmastime by giving white gifts at the Christmas Eve midnight mass. These packages hold white foods such as potatoes and rice, which will be given to the poor for their Christmas dinner. During the service, people walk forward and place gifts wrapped in white paper in a straw-filled manger. There is a light shining in the manger to symbolize the light of Christ.

Families often set out their entire Christmas Eve meal before leaving for mass so the Holy Family (Jesus, Mary, and Joseph) may come inside to eat. The weather is warm and outdoor altars are common, so midnight masses can be held outdoors.

Presebres, manger scenes, are common in most homes in this country. Children make the figures from brightly colored sawdust, and the figures are moved forward each day to commemorate the journey to Bethlehem. Other decorations include eucalyptus leaves, colorful flowers (especially red ones), fresh fruits, parrots, butterflies, and a tree covered in cotton to look like snow.

An old Brazilian legend says that on Christmas Eve, animals can speak. The rooster calls out "Christ is born!" The bull asks, "Where?" and the sheep answer, "In Bethlehem of Judea!"

In order to study Christmas in Brazil, you may wish to do some of the following activities.

ACTIVITIES

1. Brainstorm a list of "white" foods.
2. Use the proceeds from a Christmas bake sale or Brazilian flower (page 15) sale to purchase some of the items on the above list. Donate them to a local food bank. Be sure to wrap each item in white tissue paper.
3. Have a taste-testing party to sample exotic fresh fruits or white foods.
4. Make snow-covered tree ornaments. Directions can be found on page 14.
5. Make sawdust *presebres* pictures. Directions can be found on page 14.
6. Make Brazilian flowers. Directions can be found on page 15.

SNOW-COVERED TREE ORNAMENT

Materials:

- green construction paper
- tree pattern (page 126)
- cotton balls or polyester
  quilt batting
- white glue
- brightly colored
  tissue paper
- scissors
- yarn or string
- pencil

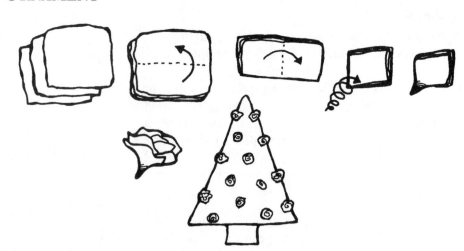

Directions:

1. Trace and cut the tree shape from green construction paper.
2. Spread a thin layer of glue over the surface of the tree.
3. Pull apart cotton balls or batting so it is in thin layers. Apply to the glued surface and press lightly.
4. To make the flowers, tear small pieces of tissue paper (approximately 2"/5 cm). Place 3–5 pieces of tissue on top of each other. Layer different colors together if desired.
5. Fold the layers of tissue in half and in half again. Grasp a folded corner and twist it to a point. This is the base of your "flower."
6. Fluff up the "petals" of the flower. Trim or fringe with scissors, if desired.
7. Glue the flowers onto the cotton-covered tree.
8. Add a loop of yarn for a hanger and suspend the tree.

SAWDUST PRESEBRES

Materials:

- tempera paints or liquid food coloring
- poster board or heavy paper
- manger scene patterns (pages 127–128)
- sawdust
- glue

Directions:

1. In a bowl, mix sawdust and coloring until the colors are pleasing. Let dry.
2. Trace patterns for a manger scene onto the poster board.
3. Run a bead of glue on all pattern lines and details you wish to emphasize.
4. Sprinkle colored sawdust as desired on the glue designs. Let each color dry before adding more glue and another color. Shake off the excess sawdust.
5. Display on a bulletin board.
6. **Option:** Make other sawdust Christmas pictures and designs using the same method.

PAPER FLOWERS

Materials:

- colorful tissue paper (5"/12.5 cm squares)
- green pipe cleaners (6"/15 cm lengths)
- scissors
- flower book or pictures for reference

Directions:

1. Look at pictures of some South American flowers.
2. Use 5 pieces of tissue paper for each flower. Stack them together and fold in half and then in half again. Then, fold diagonally so you have a triangle.
3. With scissors, cut around the outer edge in a scalloped, zig-zag, fringe, or other pattern.
4. Open up the "flower." Poke one end of a pipe cleaner through the middle of the flower and bend it over to make a small ball in the center of the flower.
5. Grasp the "stem" and base of the flower and twist them into a point to hold the stem and flower together.
6. Separate and fluff out the "petals" of the flower to look realistic.
7. Make several flowers and place them around the room or in a vase. Or, display and sell the flowers to raise money for a charity project.

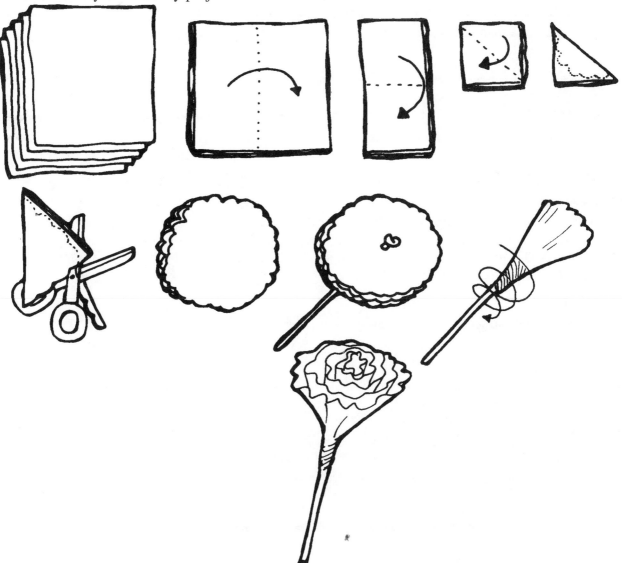

China

The biggest celebration in China is the Chinese New Year in which the people enjoy gift-giving and fireworks during the week-long holiday. However, Christmas in China is also a festive time, celebrated with very traditional customs. There are not many Christians in China, but those who are celebrate by saying, *"Sheng Tan Kuai Loh!"* Chains, flowers, and lanterns, all made of paper, are among the most popular decorations. Sometimes special paper lanterns shaped like *pagodas* (temples with pointed roofs) show a silhouette of the Holy Family inside.

One custom which is shared with other countries is the arrival of a special gift bearer. Children hang stockings and await the visit of *Lan Khoong-Khoong*, or Nice Old Father, who will fill their stockings with small gifts. He is also known as *Dun Che Lao Ren*, the Christmas Old Man.

In order to study Christmas in China, you may wish to do some of the following activities.

ACTIVITIES

1. Make and enjoy wonton cookies. The recipe below requires adult assistance.
2. Westerners enjoy Chinese fortune cookies year round. You may wish to make these with your class, but they are not a traditional Christmas custom in China today.
3. Find these Chinese Christmas carols: "Holy Night, Blessed Night" and "Midnight Stars Make Bright the Sky." Teach them to your students. (One source is the *1990 Presbyterian Hymnal.*)
4. Make a pagoda manger scene. Directions can be found on pages 17–18.

Deep-Fried Wonton Cookies

Sweet desserts are not common in China. Dessert is often fresh fruit, but on special occasions, wonton cookies are made and enjoyed. This recipe makes 2 dozen cookies.

Ingredients:

- 1½ c. (375 mL) chopped dried apples (or dates)
- 1¼ c. (315 mL) chopped dried apricots
- 1½ c. (375 mL) brown sugar
- 1½ c. (375 mL) flaked coconut
- ½ c. (125 mL) chopped almonds
- 24 wonton skins
- cooking oil in deep fat fryer
- powdered sugar (optional)

Directions:

1. Mix apples, apricots, brown sugar, coconut, and almonds in bowl.
2. Separate wonton skins and place about 2 teaspoons (10 mL) of the mixture in the center of each skin.
3. Moisten the skin edges with water and fold each skin in half diagonally to form a triangle. Press the edges together well to seal. Cover with plastic wrap while making the rest.
4. Carefully place several wontons in deep fat and fry until golden brown (1-2 minutes). (Note: This step and the following should be done by an adult.)
5. Remove the fried wontons and drain them on paper towels.
6. Cool thoroughly before eating. If desired, sprinkle with powdered sugar and serve with sherbet.

PAGODA MANGER SCENE

Materials:

- 2 pieces red tissue paper, about 8.5" x 11" (21 cm x 28 cm)
- 2½ pieces black construction paper (same as above)
- scissors
- glue
- yarn
- patterns (page 18)

Directions:

1. Cut out the pagoda pattern. Trace it onto the 2 large pieces of black construction paper. Cut out both pieces along all solid lines. These will be the pagoda frame.
2. Trace the silhouette figures of the Holy Family onto the small piece of black construction paper. Cut out.
3. Place one black pagoda frame on a flat surface. Run a bead of glue around the edge. Place one piece of red tissue paper on top of the glue. Press lightly to smooth out wrinkles.
4. Trim off excess tissue paper to match the size and shape of the frame.
5. Arrange figures as desired on top of the red tissue and glue in place.
6. Place the second piece of tissue paper on top of the figures, gluing it down around the outer edges only. Trim off the excess tissue paper.
7. Run a bead of glue around the outer edges once more, and place the second pagoda frame on top, matching all edges. Let dry.
8. Add a yarn loop from the top to hang the pagoda in a window.

Pagoda Manger Scene *(cont.)*

Czechoslovakia

December 6 is *Svaty Mikalas* Day, Czechoslovakia's version of St. Nicholas Day. The children of Czechoslovakia believe that Mikalas comes down from heaven on a golden cord. An angel in white and a devil in black (called *Cert*) come with him. As soon as he arrives, the children rush to the table and recite their prayers. If they do a good job, Svaty Mikalas instructs his angel to give them presents. If not, Cert shakes his whip and rattles his chains to remind them what may happen if they continue to be naughty.

December 24 is often called "Generous Eve." This is when a decorated evergreen tree is illuminated and gifts from family and friends are placed beneath it. The tree is decorated with various nuts, fruits, gingerbread shapes, and colored paper and fabrics. Decorated eggs, both simple and elaborate, also adorn the tree.

The holidays continue on December 25 and 26. On these days, people may enjoy seeing the *Bethlehems,* or Nativity scenes. The Bethlehems are large and quite complete, including townspeople as well as the traditional figures. They are carved from wood or shaped from bread dough, and then they are elaborately painted.

After a Christmas meal, the food is shared with the farm animals to ensure a prosperous year. Some families then practice an old fortune-telling ritual. They cut an apple in half, and if the core reveals a cross, it means something bad will happen in the coming year. If a star is revealed, it means a happy future.

In order to study Christmas in Czechoslovakia, you may wish to do some of the following activities.

ACTIVITIES

1. Wenceslaus (WEN suss luss) was a prince in Bohemia (now Czechoslovakia). The carol "Good King Wenceslaus" can be found on page 39. Learn to sing the carol. Illustrate the words.
2. Make Bethlehems. Directions can be found below.
3. Make egg ornaments. See page 20 for directions.
4. Make poppy seed cookies. See page 21 for the recipe.
5. Make houska bread. See page 21 for the recipe.

BETHLEHEMS

Materials:

- ³/₄ c. (190 mL) salt
- 3 c. (750 mL) flour
- about 1 c. (250 mL) water

Directions:

1. With a spoon, mix together the salt, flour, and water, and then use your hands to make the mixture smooth and pliable. (Yield: enough for several students to make a variety of figures.)
2. Shape tiny Bethlehem figures. If you wish to use the figures as ornaments, poke a hole in the top and insert a straightened paper clip before drying. Then, let them air dry for several days. Or, to speed the hardening process, place the figures in a 250° F (130° C) oven for 2¹/₂ hours or until completely dry. Cool.
3. Paint when dry and cool.

(You may wish to have students make figures from real bread dough. Use frozen bread dough which has been thawed. Try shaping small pieces of it, letting it rise, and baking according to directions. Do not paint! Discuss and then eat your creations.)

EGG ORNAMENT

Materials:

- plastic Easter egg
- flour
- tempera paint and small brushes
- paper towels
- pin or needle
- vaseline or oil
- water
- old Christmas cards
- scrap yarn or ribbon
- glitter (optional)
- old newspaper
- bowl and spoon
- scissors
- white craft glue

Time: This is a 2–3 day project, 20 minutes per day.

Directions:

1. Tear a newspaper into strips 1–2" (2.5–5 cm) long and no wider than 1" (2.5 cm).
2. Spread a thin layer of vaseline or oil on the egg to ease the later removal of papier-mâché.
3. Mix 1 T. (15 mL) flour with 1 T. (15 mL) water in a bowl until you have a smooth paste.
4. Dip newspaper strips into the paste, pulling them between your fingers to remove excess paste. Place over a lengthwise half of the egg. Do several layers until well covered. Let dry overnight.
5. Carefully remove the plastic egg from the papier-mâché form. You may need to loosen it around the edges with a table knife.
6. Paint inside and out with the tempera paint of your choice. Let dry.
7. Choose a design that will fit into the egg form from an old Christmas card. Cut it to the correct size and soak it in water for about 30 seconds or until softened. Lay it on an absorbent towel.
8. Place glue on back of the picture and gently insert it into the egg. Press out any wrinkles. Let it dry for a few minutes.
9. Poke a small hole in the top of the paper egg and tie ribbon or yarn on as a hanger.
10. **Optional:** Run a bead of glue around the front edge of the egg and dip it into the glitter. Shake off the excess. Let it dry.
11. Your ornament is ready to be hung on a tree!

Poppy Seed Cookies

This is a cookie version of the poppy-seed cake often served at Czechoslovakian Christmas meals. This recipe makes about 3 dozen cookies.

Ingredients:

- $\frac{1}{2}$ c. (125 mL) butter, softened
- $\frac{1}{2}$ c. (125 mL) sugar
- $\frac{1}{2}$ t. (2.5 mL) vanilla
- 1 egg
- $\frac{1}{4}$ c. (65 mL) poppy seeds (or less)
- 1 c. (250 mL) flour
- powdered sugar

Preparation:

1. Cream butter and sugar until fluffy.
2. Beat in egg and vanilla.
3. Add poppy seeds and flour and mix well.
4. Refrigerate for 1 hour or until dough can be handled.
5. Shape dough into a roll about 2" (5 cm) in diameter. Wrap tightly in plastic wrap and refrigerate for several hours.
6. Preheat oven to 325° F (170° C).
7. Unwrap roll and cut into $\frac{1}{4}$ inch (.6 cm) slices.
8. Bake on ungreased cookie sheet for 18–20 minutes.
9. Let cool slightly and remove from pan to waxed paper.
10. Sprinkle with powdered sugar.

Houska

Houska is a braided Christmas sweet bread enjoyed in Czechoslovakia.

Ingredients:

- hot roll mix or bread mix
- 2 T. (30 mL) margarine
- 3 T. (45 mL) sugar
- $\frac{1}{2}$ t. (2.5 mL) mace
- 1 c. (250 mL) raisins
- hot water
- 1 egg
- 1 t. (5 mL) grated lemon rind
- $\frac{1}{2}$ c. (125 mL) finely chopped pecans
- 1 egg beaten with 1 T. (15 mL) milk

Preparation:

1. Lightly flour a clean surface.
2. Mix hot roll mix according to the package directions but add sugar, lemon rind, and mace with hot water, margarine, and eggs.
3. Knead for 5 minutes as directed. Then knead in the nuts and raisins and let rest as directed.
4. When ready to shape, cut dough into 5 equal parts. Roll each part on a lightly floured surface into a 16" (40 cm) rope.
5. On a lightly buttered cookie sheet, line up three ropes side by side. Starting at the center of the ropes, work toward each end to braid them loosely together.
6. Twist the other two ropes together and set them lengthwise along the braided dough.
7. Tuck all ends under, cover, and let rise until doubled in size (about 20–30 minutes).
8. Preheat oven to 350° F (180° C). Brush the loaf with egg and milk mixture. Bake for 25–35 minutes or until golden brown. Remove from the oven and cool on a rack.

France

*J*oyeux *Noël* is the French way of saying, "Merry Christmas!" Indeed, in France Christmas is merry. Feasting goes with the season, and there are many good foods to be found. France may also have started the custom of giving gifts in the name of St. Nicholas, a popular custom in many countries today. The French also popularized and still give much emphasis to the crèche (kresh) or manger scene found in the Christmas story, and they have contributed some well-known carols to the Christmas season, as well. Clearly, Christmas in France is a great joy for children, for in addition to everything above, they also enjoy going to the many puppet shows and displays of animated toys seen during the holidays.

The holiday season usually begins on December 5, St. Nicholas Eve. This is one of the times for giving gifts. (French children are lucky. They might also receive gifts on Christmas Eve and New Year's Day.) Many years ago, some French nuns began leaving gifts secretly at the houses of poor families with children. These families could not afford any special things for their children, but on St. Nicholas Eve, packages of wonderful luxuries from Spain mysteriously appeared at their homes. The children might find nuts, oranges, and other wonderful fruits they had never before tasted. The gifts were credited to St. Nicholas instead of the nuns. So, now on St. Nicholas Eve, French children leave their shoes by the fireplace or radiator in the hopes that they, too, will receive some treats. Père Noël (Father Christmas) is the gift giver who visits secretly and leaves presents if they have been good. Legend tells us that a helper named Père Fouchette also visits, but he brings switches to spank the naughty children.

Sometimes on Christmas Eve, after the children are sleeping, parents hang little toys, candies, and fruits on the branches of the Christmas tree for their children to find on Christmas morning. On New Year's Day, friends and family members exchange gifts.

The Christmas tree, decorated with many stars of all colors, is found in most French homes. But it is the crèche that is the center of the celebration. (The crèche originated in Italy but has become an important tradition in France.) A few days before Christmas, the family takes great care in assembling their crèche. The children choose the spot in the home where the crèche will be placed. The figures in the crèche are called *santons* and are often hand-made from clay. The last figure placed within the crèche is baby Jesus (le Petit Noël). Evergreens and candles decorate the crèche, and then the family sings carols around it in celebration of Christ's birth.

Some famous French carols include "The First Noël" which was originally a shepherd's tune, "Angels from the Realms of Glory," and "O Come, O Come, Immanuel." Bells often ring out with these songs.

Wonderful foods abound at Christmas. Many French people fast during the day of December 24, but after a midnight church service, they eat a réveillon supper of ham, fowl, salads, cakes, and other sweets. Fresh goose is a tradition because legend says the Three Wise Men were met by geese when they arrived at the manger. Christmas Day is another day of feasting with family members, and the meal always includes a crusty French bread. *Bûche de Noël* is a traditional cake which looks like a Yule log. Two other days of feasting during the holiday occur on New Year's Day and Epiphany. On Epiphany, the French often bake a Twelfth Night Cake called *Galette des Rois*. There is a bean or tiny china doll baked inside, and the finder becomes the king or queen for the day. He or she may choose a partner, and the couple wears crowns as the group sings, dances, watches plays, and eats.

In order to study Christmas in France, you may wish to do some of the following activities.

ACTIVITIES

1. Read "The Miracle of the Fir Trees" by Jean Variot. A nice version is in *An American Christmas* illustrated by Emily Boland. Ask your students to make illustrations and display them.

2. Give a puppet show. Divide the class into small groups and let them decide on a story or play they would like to share. You may want to use the library as a resource, or perhaps the students would like to write a short play themselves. Using paper lunch sacks, yarn, fabric, and markers, create characters that can be used to perform the puppet show. Cover a table with a large blanket to use as the stage. Practice! When the groups are ready, perform the puppet shows.

3. Set up a *crèche* and *santons de provence*. (See below and page 24.) Let your students decide where to place it, and make construction paper holly and ivy decorations to surround it. Sing some French Christmas carols while gathered around the crèche. (See page 26.)

4. Plant grain in small dishes. Tradition says if it sprouts and grows before Christmas, it means a bountiful harvest in the coming year. Chart the time and progress of the growth.

5. Make *colombes* or *galette des rois*. See the recipes on page 25.

CRÈCHE AND SANTONS DE PROVENCE

The directions below and on the next page will show how to make a crèche and santons de provence (little saints of Provence). Make modeling clay following the recipe here or use commercial clay. Then let the students create figures to use with the crèche. Figures may be left white, painted, or "dressed" using yarn, foil, pipe cleaners, fabric, or felt scraps. Pencil, pen, or permanent markers will work to provide facial features.

Crèche Materials:

- shoebox
- glue
- straw, yellow yarn, or wood shavings
- evergreen branches
- poster board
- brown marker or crayon
- scissors
- modeling dough
- gold foil or yellow construction paper
- clear plastic straw
- tape

Crèche Directions:

1. Use the shoebox without its lid to represent the stable. Set it on its side and decorate inside and out by gluing on pieces of straw, yellow yarn, or wood shavings as well as evergreen branches.

2. Use the poster board to make the manger. Cut a 3" x 4" (7.5 cm x 10 cm) rectangle from the poster board and fold it in half. Tape a 2" (5 cm) strip across the sides to hold them open in a V shape. Color with brown marker or crayons. Fill with pieces of straw or yellow yarn.

3. Use the modeling clay recipe below to create the figures for the crèche. Include the Holy Family, an angel, animals, shepherds, and the Three Wise Men. The latter can be added on January 6, Epiphany.

4. Form a star from gold foil or yellow construction paper. Attach to one end of a clear plastic straw and mount it on the back of the stable with tape.

CRÈCHE AND SANTONS DE PROVENCE *(cont.)*

Salt Dough Materials:
- 2 c. (500 mL) salt
- 1 c. (250 mL) cornstarch
- food coloring (optional)
- $^2/_3$ c. (170 mL) water
- $^1/_2$ c. (125 mL) cold water

Salt Dough Directions:
1. Mix the salt and $^2/_3$ c. (170 mL) water in a saucepan. (To color, add food coloring to water before mixing.) Stir over medium heat for 4-5 minutes.
2. Remove from heat. Add cornstarch and cold water.
3. Stir until smooth and return to heat.
4. Cook until it is thick and pulls away from the sides of the pan.
5. Cool dough until you can handle it.
6. The dough dries out rather quickly, so use it as soon as possible. It is somewhat sparkly and translucent when dry. It can be painted and decorated or left white. Encourage the students to make very simple forms and shapes.
7. When the figures have been made, let them dry and harden for several days.

Cornstarch Dough materials:
- 1 c. (250 mL) cornstarch
- 2 c. (500 mL) baking soda
- $1^1/_4$ c. (310 mL) water
- food coloring (optional)

Cornstarch Dough Directions:
1. Mix all ingredients in a saucepan.
2. Cook over medium heat to dough-like consistency, stirring constantly. Do *not* overcook. Remove from heat.
3. When cool, turn mixture out on pastry board and knead for two minutes.
4. Cover with a damp cloth, or keep in an air-tight container. Best if used promptly. Will harden in 3–5 days.

Note: To make more clay, prepare another batch. Do not double the recipe.

Santons de Provence Materials:
- salt or cornstarch dough (or see page 19)
- toothpicks
- water

Santons de Provence Directions:
1. Mold the dough into figures and shapes as desired. Adult santon figures should be about 4 inches (10 cm) high. The baby should be the size of the manger, and the animals should be made in proportion to the other figures. It is helpful to shape figures by molding the body and head from one piece, but students may prefer to try other methods. Be sure the base is broad and flat. Toothpicks can be inserted to stabilize any long narrow pieces of dough, for example, the camel's neck. Use a few drops of water and pinch the dough if necessary to hold intersecting pieces together. Sitting characters can be shaped using a wooden block or old film canister for a "chair."
2. Do not forget to make interesting accessories, such as pipe cleaner shepherds' crooks and foil crowns and gifts for the kings. The figures may also be dressed using simple fabric "shawls," "skirts," or "ponchos."

Colombes

These special dove cookies are a French Christmas treat.

Ingredients and Materials:
- ³/₄ c. (190 mL) butter (slightly softened)
- 1 egg
- 1¹/₂ t. (7.5 mL) baking powder
- chocolate chips or raisins
- 6 T. (90 mL) sugar
- 1¹/₂ c. (375 mL) flour
- 2-3 T. (30–45 mL) milk

Preparation:
1. Combine butter, sugar, and egg. Mix well.
2. Mix baking powder into flour and add dry ingredients to the creamed mixture.
3. Knead thoroughly, adding milk 1 T. at a time until you get a smooth, stiff dough.
4. Chill for several hours.
5. Heat the oven to 375° F (190° C).
6. Roll the dough out to 1/4" (.6 cm) thickness with a floured rolling pin on a floured work surface. Cut the dough with a bird-shaped cookie cutter or use a knife around the pattern on page 129. Place on an ungreased cookie sheet.
7. Add a raisin or chocolate chip to each cookie for an eye.
8. Bake for about 10 minutes until golden. Cool slightly and remove from the pan.

Galette des Rois

Galette des Rois is enjoyed by the French on Epiphany. A bean or tiny china doll is baked inside the cake, and the finder becomes the king or queen for the day.

Ingredients:
- 2 sheets frozen puff pastry (thawed for 20 minutes)
- ¹/₈ t. (.6 mL) almond extract
- 1 egg
- 3¹/₂ oz. (100 g) almond paste
- 3 t. (15 mL) sugar
- 1 dried bean or tiny china doll

Preparation:
1. In a bowl, break up almond paste. Lightly flour a clean work surface. Preheat the oven to 425° F (220° C).
2. Beat the egg with a fork. Mix 1 T. egg and the extract with the paste until smooth.
3. Unfold 1 pastry on the floured surface. Cut it into a circle approximately 8" (20 cm) in diameter. Place on an ungreased cookie sheet. Also cut the remaining pastry, but set aside.
4. Spread the almond filling on the first pastry round to within ³/₄ inch (2 cm) of the cut edges.
5. Lightly press the dried bean or doll into the dough somewhere.
6. Brush beaten egg along the cut edges of the first pastry. Try not to get it on the cookie sheet.
7. Carefully lift the second pastry sheet and place it on top of the first, aligning the edges.
8. Press the top and bottom edges together with a fork or rounded end of a table knife to seal.
9. Brush the remaining beaten egg over the top. With a knife point, draw 5 or 6 indented lines across the top in one direction and then at right angles, creating a checkered appearance.
10. Sprinkle sugar on top and bake for 20 minutes until the dough puffs up and is golden. Cool.

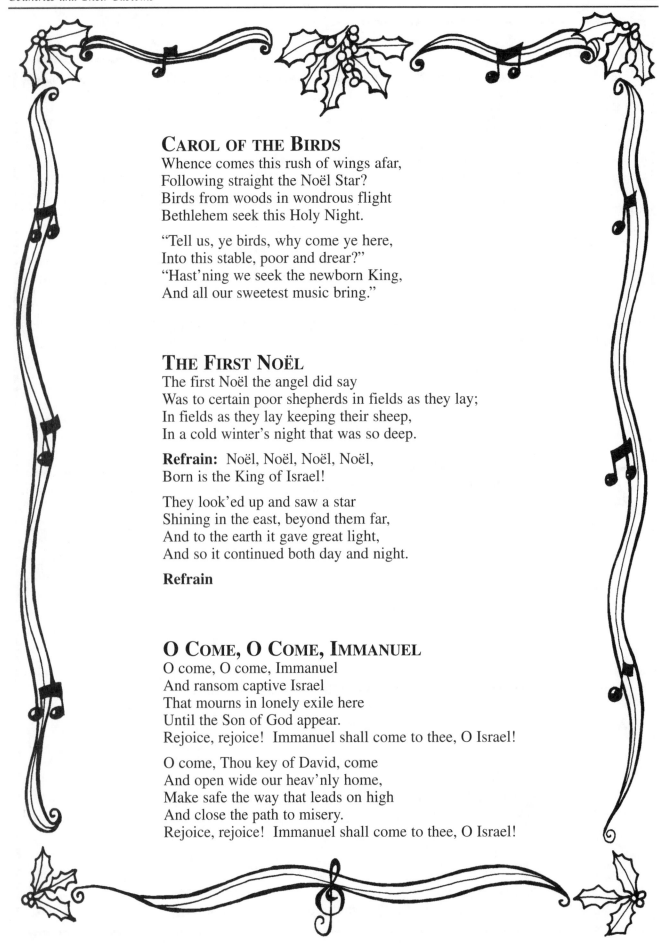

CAROL OF THE BIRDS

Whence comes this rush of wings afar,
Following straight the Noël Star?
Birds from woods in wondrous flight
Bethlehem seek this Holy Night.

"Tell us, ye birds, why come ye here,
Into this stable, poor and drear?"
"Hast'ning we seek the newborn King,
And all our sweetest music bring."

THE FIRST NOËL

The first Noël the angel did say
Was to certain poor shepherds in fields as they lay;
In fields as they lay keeping their sheep,
In a cold winter's night that was so deep.

Refrain: Noël, Noël, Noël, Noël,
Born is the King of Israel!

They look'ed up and saw a star
Shining in the east, beyond them far,
And to the earth it gave great light,
And so it continued both day and night.

Refrain

O COME, O COME, IMMANUEL

O come, O come, Immanuel
And ransom captive Israel
That mourns in lonely exile here
Until the Son of God appear.
Rejoice, rejoice! Immanuel shall come to thee, O Israel!

O come, Thou key of David, come
And open wide our heav'nly home,
Make safe the way that leads on high
And close the path to misery.
Rejoice, rejoice! Immanuel shall come to thee, O Israel!

Germany

Frohliche Weihnachten! That is how the Germans say, "Merry Christmas!" The German people have long loved Christmas. Together with the Irish in America, they are credited with convincing the staid and serious Puritans that Christmas could be celebrated merrily without betraying the importance of the Sabbath.

The Christmas tree as we know it today probably began as a German custom in the sixteenth century. According to legend, Martin Luther, a leader of Protestant church reform, was the first to bring an evergreen tree indoors. While outside on Christmas Eve, he became so moved by the beauty of the tall trees against the starry sky, that he cut one down and brought it home to his family. He placed lighted candles on the boughs to symbolize the stars sparkling over Bethlehem.

"O Tannenbaum" is a popular German Christmas carol based on the tree custom. Originally the trees were small enough to set on a table. They were decorated with red apples, cookies, candies, and candles. Since lit candles on a tree can be hazardous, families would light them only on Christmas Eve.

The popularity of the Christmas tree spread to royalty in France and England. They added an angel on top and toys underneath. It was not long before the middle-class people wanted trees, too. Today, Christmas trees are one of the most popular Christmas customs and symbols, though electric lights have replaced the candles. Christmas trees can be found everywhere.

Who brings gifts to little German children? There are different names and gift bearers in different parts of Germany. In northern Germany, it is *Pelze Nicol* (fur-clad Nicholas) or *Buller Clos* (Nicholas with bells). Each is a helper or servant to *Kirst Kindl* or *Christkindl,* the Christ Child. The gifts of the Christ Child are brought by a young child dressed in white wearing a golden crown decorated with lighted candles. He holds a little fir tree. In other parts of Germany, the gift bearer is called *Kriss Kringle* or *Weihnachtsmann* (Christmas Man), and he may arrive by mule or white horse. He peeks in a window to check on the children as they sleep. Before going to bed, they set out plates of cookies and nuts for him and leave straw, hay, or carrots for the animal. If the children have been good, they will find small gifts in their shoes when they awaken, or in some places, their gifts will be found among the tree branches. However, if they have been naughty, a mean fellow called *Hans Trapp* will pay them a visit. He travels as a "servant" to Kriss Kringle, but he delivers only tree switches meant for spankings!

Germany is famous for a huge toy fair held in Nuremberg early each December. It is called *Christkindlesmarkt.* Shoppers find toys and gifts of every kind as well as glass ornaments, marzipan candies, and gingerbread figures. This is a festive place with music everywhere.

In the four weeks prior to Christmas, families use an Advent wreath and light one candle each Sunday, including a fifth on Christmas Day. But the main celebration for the German family takes place on Christmas Eve. Children are allowed to stay up late, for this is the time to decorate the tree, go to church, eat a traditional meal, sing carols, and exchange family gifts.

ACTIVITIES

1. Read "The Little Stranger" to your class. A nice version is found in *The Solstice Evergreen.* The story tells a version of the Christ child's gift of the fir tree, a symbol for happiness.
2. A nice Christmas tree story with a lesson on sharing is found in *Our Christmas Book* by Jane Belk Moncure. It is most appropriate for early elementary age students.

ACTIVITIES *(cont.)*

3. Have the students illustrate the meaning of the song "O Christmas Tree" (page 31). They can also define the following words from the song: boughs, base, summit, splendor, and unchanging.

4. Write new words to fit the tune of "O Christmas Tree."

5. Make a Christmas tree centerpiece. See below for directions.

6. Research to discover more about evergreen trees. Discuss the environmental issue of cutting down trees for Christmas. (See page 109 for more about Christmas greenery.)

7. In early December, set up your own Christkindlesmarkt. Make and sell sweet treats and small student-made toys and ornaments. Use the activity to teach simple marketing, sales, and accounting skills. As a class, decide on a charitable use for the proceeds from the sale. Practice the expression of generosity!

8. The traditional gingerbread house and figures came from Germany. Make gingerbread figures by using the recipe on page 30.

CHRISTMAS TREE CENTERPIECE

Materials:

- pattern (page 29)
- white plastic straws
- craft glue and tape
- toothpicks
- red, green, and yellow tissue paper
- cardboard from recycled cereal boxes (trimmed by teacher)
- scissors
- gold or silver star stickers

Directions:

1. Cut out the pattern and trace it onto a piece of cardboard. Cut out the cardboard shape.

2. Form a cone with the cardboard shape, and overlap and tape the edges securely. Trim off the bottom edge if necessary so the cone stands up straight on a flat surface.

3. **Teacher:** Cut green tissue paper into long strips, 6" (15 cm) wide. Each student will need 3-5 strips. **Students:** Fold each strip in thirds lengthwise. Now each strip is only 2" (5 cm) wide. Use scissors to make vertical cuts along the length of the strips. Cut to within ¹/₂" (1.25 cm) of the top edge.

4. Starting at the bottom of the cone, wrap a strip around the cone so the cut edge flares out. Tape or glue the upper edge of the tissue paper to the cone as you wind it upwards on the cone. Repeat with each strip, layering them so at least ¹/₂" (1.25 cm) of fringe shows on each strip. Continue to the top of the cone. Trim and secure the tissue at the tip.

5. Take two star stickers and place them back-to-back around the top of a toothpick. Insert the toothpick into the top of the cone.

6. **Teacher:** Cut red tissue paper into many 4" (10 cm) squares. **Students:** Wad up the squares of red tissue paper to represent apples. Glue them onto your tree.

7. Cut straws into eight ³/₄" (2 cm) lengths to represent candles. Tear and twist a tiny scrap of yellow tissue. Glue one end of the tissue "flame" into one end of the "candle" piece. Glue these candles onto the tree. Enjoy!

CHRISTMAS TREE CENTERPIECE PATTERN

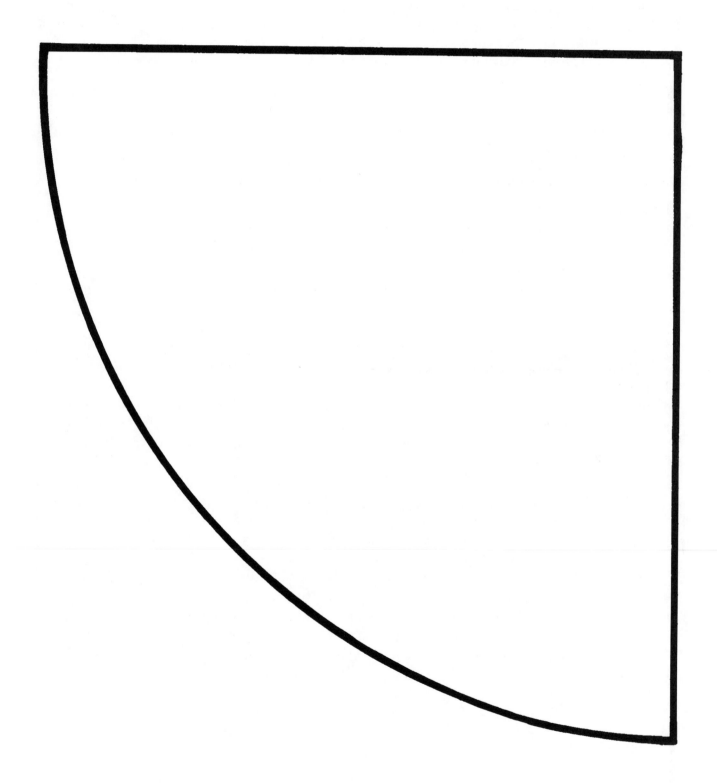

Gingerbread People

The Germans originated the traditional Christmas gingerbread house and figures. These cookies can be made into decorations for a Christmas tree. Depending on the size of the cookie cutters, the recipe makes about 4 dozen cookies.

Ingredients:

- $\frac{1}{2}$ c. (125 mL) shortening
- $\frac{1}{2}$ c. (125 mL) butter, softened
- $\frac{1}{4}$ c. (65 mL) granulated sugar
- 1 c. (250 mL) brown sugar
- 1 egg
- $\frac{1}{2}$ c. (125 mL) dark molasses
- 4 c. (1000 mL) flour
- 1 t. (5 mL) baking soda

- $1\frac{1}{2}$ t. (7.5 mL) ground cinnamon
- 1 t. (5 mL) ground ginger
- $\frac{1}{4}$ t. (1.25 mL) ground cloves
- $\frac{1}{4}$ t. (1.25 mL) ground allspice
- $\frac{1}{4}$ t. (1.25 mL) salt
- 1 T. (15 mL) white vinegar
- ready-to-spread frosting
- raisins, red candies, and other decorations

Preparation:

1. With electric mixer, cream shortening, butter, and sugars together.
2. Add egg, molasses, and vinegar, and continue to beat until fluffy.
3. In a separate bowl, stir together flour, soda, and all seasonings.
4. Add dry ingredients to the batter mixture and mix on a low speed until well blended.

Gingerbread People *(cont.)*

Preparation: *(cont.)*

5. Cover with plastic wrap and place in the refrigerator for 2 hours or more to chill the dough.
6. Preheat the oven to 325° F (170° C). Prepare a well-floured rolling surface.
7. Take about a $\frac{1}{4}$ portion of the dough. Roll it out on the floured surface to about $\frac{1}{4}$" (.6 cm) thickness. Cut with cookie cutters.
8. Use a spatula to pick up the dough cookies carefully and place them on a baking sheet. Allow a little space between the cookies.
9. If you plan to hang the cookies on a tree, poke a hole in the top of each with a small straw.
10. Bake for about 8 minutes.
11. Cool slightly, and then remove from the baking sheet and cool completely on waxed paper.
12. Decorate with frosting, raisins, red candies, or other decorations as desired.
13. To hang, thread yarn, ribbon, or nylon thread through the hole you made and tie it into a loop.

O TANNENBAUM! *(German)*

O Tannenbaum, O Tannenbaum!
Wie treu sind deine Blätter!
Du grünst nicht nur in Sommerzeit,
Nein, auch im Winter, wenn es schneit.
O Tannenbaum, O Tannenbaum!
Wie treu sind deine Blatter!

O CHRISTMAS TREE! *(English)*

O Christmas tree, O Christmas tree!
With faithful leaves unchanging;
Not only green in summer's heat,
But also winter's snow and sleet.
O Christmas tree, O Christmas tree!
With faithful leaves unchanging.

Great Britain
(England, Ireland, Scotland, and Wales)

Happy Christmas! is the traditional English Christmas greeting. Many of the most popular Christmas customs in the world today come from Great Britain. For example, the Christmas card originated in England, and some think that school children were the first to send them. Away from home attending school, they would make and send beautiful cards informing their parents of their progress and hinting that gift-giving season was near. The first Christmas card was printed in England in 1843, and its popularity grew.

"Wassailing" is also a British custom. Groups of people walk up and down the streets of their neighborhoods at Christmastime singing carols while sipping a hot punch-like drink. The children in the group hope to receive treats while they sing. Wassail means "be in good health," and when a group of people drink wassail together, all quarreling is supposed to end. Sometimes farmers even wassailed their livestock and fields to ensure a successful year! Wassailing takes place most commonly during the twelve days of Christmas (between Christmas and January 6). Traditionally, this whole period is a time of great revelry.

England's gift giver is Father Christmas. He is tall, slender, dressed in red, and sporting a long white beard. Children write letters to him listing their gift requests. Sometimes they toss these letters into the fireplace. If the letter is carried up the chimney by the draft, their wishes will come true. If the letter burns, they must try again. Father Christmas arrives on a white donkey or white horned goat and may carry a bowl of wassail. He used to go from home to home during the twelve days of Christmas. Today, most English children hang stockings by the fireplace and will receive their gifts on Christmas afternoon.

"Mumming" is another English tradition. People dress in costumes and masks to put on Christmas plays throughout the holiday season. Sometimes Father Christmas joins in the festivities, too.

Holly, ivy, and mistletoe are also important parts of an English holiday. Children used to search the woods for branches of holly to decorate their home. The carol "Deck the Halls with Boughs of Holly" reflects this tradition. If a girl is kissed beneath a bunch of mistletoe, she is given one berry from the plant to bring her good luck. When the berries are gone, so are the kisses!

Before the English have their Christmas feast, they pull open Christmas "crackers." These are paper cylinders filled with small prizes and riddles. They make a noisy cracking sound when opened. Sometimes they include paper hats which are to be worn around the holiday dinner table.

Dinner often includes twelve or more courses. The most popular foods are roast goose, roast beef, Yorkshire pudding, and plum pudding, which is like a heavy cake. Mincemeat pies used to be made from a variety of meats such as rabbit and pheasant, but now they only contain minced dried fruits. Often there are sugar statues of the Wise Men or the Holy Family set on the table for dessert. These are called "subtleties." Special holiday foods also include Scottish shortbread and Irish griddle cakes.

After dinner, the family goes to a sitting room to tell ghost stories or "Christmas Tales." The most famous tale is Charles Dickens' *A Christmas Carol*. There may be a Yule log in the fireplace, although this is not as large as it was many years ago. In many homes today, candles have replaced blazing fires to represent the Star of Bethlehem and the Light of the World.

Boxing Day in England is on December 26. In the past, people rewarded their good servants with gifts of money enclosed inside special boxes that were opened on the day after Christmas. Today, this public holiday is still celebrated, but the "Christmas boxes" are given to community workers such as mail carriers.

ACTIVITIES

1. Read "The Twelve Days of Christmas" to your students. One nice version is found in *The Doubleday Christmas Treasury*. Compare different versions and define words the students do not understand. Then have groups of students write their own contemporary versions entitled "The Twelve Days of Christmas in _____." In the blank, list the year, class, or city.

2. Ghostly Christmas stories were popular in England. Share some of these with your students, and then ask them to write their own ghost stories with a Christmas theme. Illustrate them and put them in the school library to be shared with other classes.

3. Practice the art of mumming. Write a Christmas play and perform it for parents, using costumes and masks.

4. Take a field trip to a card or print shop to learn more about the production of Christmas cards. Also tour a post office to find out about the delivery of the mail. (Note: In the meantime, learn or review the proper procedure for addressing an envelope.)

5. Make Christmas crackers. Directions can be found on page 34.

6. Make gift boxes. Directions can be found on pages 34–35.

7. Make Christmas cards. Directions can be found on page 36.

8. Play an English Christmas game. Three hundred years ago, children in England played a game with mistletoe—and it had nothing to do with kissing! To play, you will need a piece of mistletoe, a shoe, and a group of children.

   Hang the mistletoe from the ceiling. Have the children hold hands to form a circle beneath the mistletoe. One player tosses the shoe into the center of the circle. The player aims the shoe so it will land under the mistletoe. If it does not land under the mistletoe, the shoe is passed to the next person to try. If it does land correctly, everyone looks to see to whom the shoe points. That person must try to run to the shoe and pick it up before being tagged by the one who tossed it. If tagged before picking up the shoe, that player tosses the shoe next. If not tagged, then the original player tosses again.

9. Make wassail. A recipe can be found on page 36.

10. Make plum pudding. A recipe can be found on page 37.

11. Make pomander balls. To do so, each child will need one whole orange, whole cloves, and ribbon or yarn. Push whole cloves into the orange peel until the entire orange is "studded." Tie ribbon around the ball to make a sling and leave a length for hanging it. Set it aside for several weeks to dry. (Optional: Place it inside a nylon bag to dry more evenly.) Tighten the yarn hanger as necessary and hang in a room or closet for a wonderful scent.

12. Some famous English Christmas carols are included on pages 38 and 39. Learn the songs, and then ask the students how they reflect English Christmas traditions.

13. Have the students retell and illustrate the story of "Good King Wenceslas."

CHRISTMAS CRACKER

Materials:

- cardboard toilet paper tube
- tissue or crepe paper sheet (any color)
- two 12" (30 cm) lengths of yarn
- small toys or wrapped candies
- small scrap of paper
- pen or pencil
- tape or glue (optional)

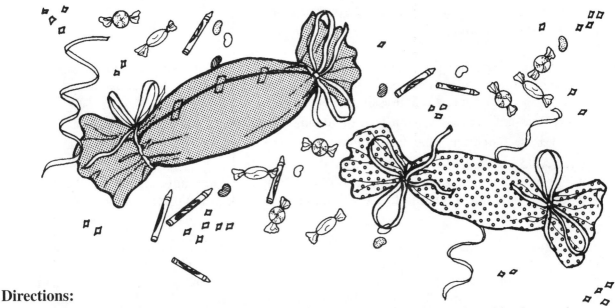

Directions:

1. On the scrap of paper, write a riddle, joke, or lesson (moral) to be enclosed in the cracker.
2. Cut colored paper into 7" x 12" (17.5 cm x 30 cm) pieces.
3. Roll the cardboard tube in tissue paper. Tape or glue if desired.
4. With yarn, tie a tight bow in one end and fan out the remaining paper.
5. Place the riddle and toys or candies inside the tube.
6. Use yarn to tie up the other end.
7. When the Christmas celebration begins, children may yank both ends to pull open the cylinders and discover their treats!

GIFT BOX

Materials:

- pattern (page 35)
- heavy paper
- scissors
- markers, stickers, etc. for decoration
- yarn or ribbon
- clear transparent tape

Directions:

1. Duplicate the gift box pattern on a variety of colored paper.
2. Let the students choose a color they like and add decorations before putting it together.
3. Cut and fold the box according to the steps listed on the pattern page.
4. After inserting a small gift item, tie the box closed with ribbon or yarn. Give it to a friend!

GIFT BOX PATTERN

Cut out around the solid lines. Fold along each dotted line. With the box bottom on the table top, bring the flaps and sides upright. Glue or tape the flaps on the inside, overlapping so the creases align.

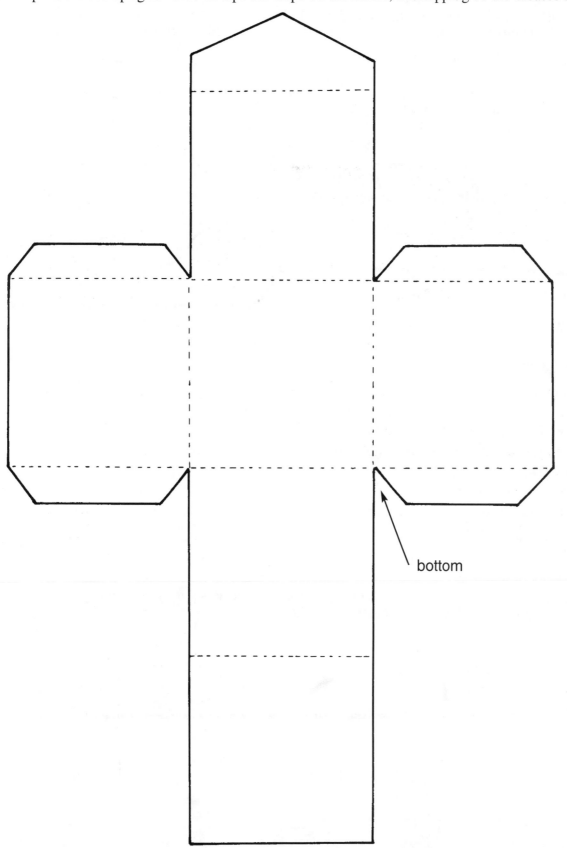

bottom

CHRISTMAS CARD

Traditional symbols on Christmas cards are roses, cupids, birds, winter scenes, Christmas greenery, family gatherings, and Father Christmas. Some cards of old were serious while others told jokes.

Post some old cards around the room for stimulus, and let students create some of their own cards using construction paper. Cut them to fit old envelopes you have collected. Let students use markers, puff paints, glitter, fabrics, trims, and stencils as desired. Have a brainstorming session to help students decide to whom the cards can be sent. (If postage money is a problem, hand deliver the cards to residents of a nursing home, veterans' home, or other similar locations.) School personnel always enjoy cards, too!

Wassail

"Wassailing" is an English custom. Groups of people walk up and down the streets of their neighborhoods at Christmastime singing carols while sipping this hot, punch-like drink.

Ingredients:
- 1 gallon (4 L) apple cider
- 1 whole clove per child (20–35)
- 1 whole allspice per child (20–35)
- 2–3 sticks cinnamon
- $^2/_3$ cup (165 mL) sugar
- 1–2 sliced oranges or apples (optional)

Preparation:
Put cider in a 30-cup electric coffee pot or a covered large pot on a hot plate. Have students add the spices and sugar. Simmer the mixture about 30 minutes. Strain out all spices and pour into a punch bowl to serve. Orange slices may be added to float on top. Serve in insulated cups and wish each other, "Good health!"

Plum Pudding

Plum pudding is a traditional English dessert. It is not really a pudding but rather a cake. It can also be rather difficult to make!

Ingredients:

- 4 slices white bread (cubed)
- 2 eggs (slightly beaten)
- 3 T. (45 mL) orange juice
- 1 t. (5 mL) vanilla
- 1 t. (5 mL) baking soda
- 2 t. (10 mL) ground cinnamon
- ½ t. (2.5 mL) ground mace
- 1 c. (250 mL) chopped dates
- ½ c. (125 mL) chopped walnuts

- 1 c. (250 mL) milk
- 1 c. (250 mL) brown sugar
- 5 T. (75 mL) butter (cut into small pieces)
- 1 c. (250 mL) flour
- ½ t. (2.5 mL) salt
- 1 t. (5 mL) ground cloves
- 2 c. (500 mL) raisins
- ½ c. (125 mL) candied fruits and peels, chopped

Preparation:

1. Grease a 2-quart (2-liter) heat-proof mold. You will need a Dutch oven or large steamer, also. Boil several cups of water in another saucepan.
2. Soak bread cubes in milk for 5 minutes, then beat together.
3. Stir in eggs, sugar, juice, butter, and vanilla.
4. Mix flour, soda, salt, and spices together. Add to the bread mixture.
5. Stir in raisins, dates, candied fruits, and nuts. Mix well.

Plum Pudding *(cont.)*

6. Pour mixture into greased mold. Cover first with lightly greased wax paper and then tightly with heavy-duty foil. Tie with a string. Put on the metal lid of the mold.
7. Place mold on the rack in the Dutch oven or steamer. Add boiling water to the steamer to come about ⅓ of the way up the mold. Cover tightly.
8. Keep water boiling gently over a low heat for approximately 3½ hours. Add more water if necessary, but do not remove the lid too often.
9. Remove mold from steamer and cool the pudding for 10 minutes. Loosen the pudding from the mold by running a knife around the edges. Remove from the mold by inverting the mold onto a serving plate.
10. Serve warm with hard sauce (below). The sauce will melt on the warm cake.

Hard Sauce

Ingredients:

- ½ c. (125 mL) butter
- 3 t. (15 mL) vanilla
- 1½ c. (375 mL) powdered sugar
- 4 t. (20 mL) water

Directions:

1. Cream butter until fluffy.
2. Beat in powdered sugar, vanilla, and water.
3. Put into refrigerator to chill before using.
4. Serve on top of warm plum pudding.

THE WASSAIL SONG

Here we come a-wassailing
Among the leaves so green.
Here we come a-wandering,
So fair to be seen.

Refrain: Love and joy come to you,
And to you your wassail too,
And God bless you, and send you
A happy new year,
And God send you a happy new year.

We are not daily beggars
That beg from door to door,
But we are neighbors' children
Whom you have seen before.

Refrain

WE WISH YOU A MERRY CHRISTMAS

We wish you a Merry Christmas,
We wish you a Merry Christmas,
We wish you a Merry Christmas
And a Happy New Year!

Glad tidings we bring
To you and your kin.
We wish you a Merry Christmas
And a Happy New Year.

Oh, bring us some figgy pudding,
Oh, bring us some figgy pudding,
Oh, bring us some figgy pudding
And a glass of good cheer!

We won't go until we get some,
We won't go until we get some,
We won't go until we get some
So bring it right here!

(Repeat the first verse.)

GOOD KING WENCESLAS

Good King Wenceslas look'd out
On the Feast of Stephen.
When the snow lay round about,
Deep, and crisp, and even;
Brightly shone the moon that night
Tho' the frost was cruel,
When a poor man came in sight,
Gath'ring winter fuel.

"Hither page, and stand by me,
If thou know'st telling,
Yonder peasant, who is he?
Where, and what his dwelling?"
"Sire, he lives a good league hence,
Underneath the mountain;
Right against the forest fence,
By St. Agnes' fountain."

"Bring me flesh and bring me wine,
Bring me pine logs hither;
Thou and I will see him dine
When we bear them hither."
Page and monarch forth they went,
Forth they went together
Through the rude wind's wild lament
And the bitter weather.

DECK THE HALLS

Deck the halls with boughs of holly,
Fa la la la la, la la la la.
'Tis the season to be jolly,
Fa la la la la, la la la la.
Don we now our gay apparel,
Fa la la, la la la, la la la.
Troll the ancient Yuletide carol,
Fa la la la la, la la la la.
See the blazing yule before us,
Fa la la la la, la la la la.
Strike the harp, and join the chorus,
Fa la la la la, la la la la.
Follow me in merry measure,
Fa la la, la la la, la la la.
While I tell of Christmas treasure,
Fa la la la la, la la la la.
Fast away the old year passes,
Fa la la la la, la la la la.
Hail the new! ye lads and lasses,
Fa la la la la, la la la la.
Sing we joyous all together,
Fa la la, la la la, la la la.
Heedless of the wind and weather,
Fa la la la la, la la la la.

Greece

Christmas in Greece is greeted with a hearty *"Eftihismena Christougenna!"* The celebration begins on December 6, the Feast of St. Nicholas. However, it is St. Basil, the patron saint of the poor and homeless, who delivers gifts on his feast day, January 1. St. Basil's Day is a bigger celebration in Greece than is Christmas. Legend tells of Basil's gift to poor girls. He is said to have tossed special cakes called *vasilopita* through their windows. Inside the cake, each found a coin providing the dowry needed to marry. Today, vasilopita are baked on St. Basil's Eve, and the person who finds the coin is supposed to have good luck in the coming year.

On Christmas Eve, a special bread called *christpomo* (Christ bread) is set in the middle of the table with a pot of honey and a cornucopia full of dried fruits and nuts. The master of the house blesses the bread with the sign of the cross and gives each person a slice. The family lifts the table three times and then eats. On Christmas Day, groups of children go from house to house singing *kalanda,* carols that tell of Christ's birth and wish well the people in each home.

Another legend tells of the *Kallikantzaroi,* goblins who come from dark places and make mischief between December 25 and January 6. To ward off their visits, a fire burns in the fireplace night and day. When Epiphany arrives, the Kallikantzaroi disappear into the darkness. A priest tosses a small cross into the sea, thereby giving hope for the renewal of light and spring.

ACTIVITIES

1. Rewrite the legends of St. Basil or the Kallikantzaroi. Include illustrations.
2. Make Greek butter cookies to celebrate the season

Butter Cookies

These treats are eaten year-round, but at Christmas time whole cloves decorate the tops to symbolize the spices brought by the Wise Men.

Ingredients:

- 1 c. (250 mL) butter (softened)
- 1 egg
- ½ t. (2.5 mL) almond extract
- 1 t. (5 mL) baking powder
- whole cloves
- ½ c. (125 mL) sugar
- ½ t. (2.5 mL) vanilla extract
- 2½ c. (625 mL) flour
- ¼ t. (1.25 mL) salt
- powdered sugar

Preparation:

1. With an electric mixer, beat together the butter, sugar, and egg until fluffy.
2. In a separate bowl, mix flour, baking powder, and salt.
3. Add these dry ingredients to the creamed mixture. Blend thoroughly.
4. Stir in vanilla and almond extracts. Mix well.
5. Using your hands, shape dough into balls, crescents, or S shapes. Use about 1 T. (15 mL) dough (or less) for each cookie.
6. Place cookies 2" (5 cm) apart on a shiny cookie sheet. Press whole cloves into the tops of the cookies if desired.
7. Bake at 350° F (180° C) for about 15 minutes or until barely golden around the edges.
8. Remove from the cookie sheet while warm. Let cool for 5 minutes.
9. Sprinkle a thin layer of powdered sugar over the tops of the cookies, using a sifter or sieve.

Italy

*M*erry *Christmas* in Italian is *Buon Natale!* Christmastime is merry for the people of Italy, but their long religious history also makes it a solemn occasion. The first manger scene was made in Italy by St. Francis of Assisi so that others might worship the infant Jesus. Italy and St. Francis are also credited with the first true Christmas carols, and, of course, Italy is renowned for its deeply religious paintings of the Holy Family.

Italians begin their holiday on the first Sunday in Advent when stores begin to display Christmas sweets such as *torrone.* The period of nine days before Christmas Day is called the novena, and this is a very festive time. Bagpipers dressed in sheepskins perform in the streets. Children walk from house to house reciting Christmas verses in exchange for coins. There are lively Christmas fairs complete with fireworks, bonfires, carols sung by shepherds, and an abundance of lights.

The Italian manger scene is called a *presepio.* Presepios are set up in the weeks before Christmas in every church and most homes. Some are miniatures carved from wood while others are life-sized, filling a room or front yard. Some are elaborate and include items like fountains and streams. But in every presepio, the manger remains empty until Christmas Eve. On that night, as the family gathers around, the Christ Child figure is passed from person to person. With songs and prayers, he is placed in the manger. The family then eats a meatless supper, *pranzo della vigilia,* which may include seafoods such as eel, cod, squid, octopus, and clams.

At ten o'clock in the evening, Christmas Eve masses begin. Afterwards, children go to sleep. Although the traditional time for children to receive gifts is January 6, many families today have adopted the custom of receiving gifts on Christmas Eve as well. To maintain the religious aspects so important to Italy, these gifts may come from *Gesú Bambino* (Baby Jesus). However, in some homes Santa may deliver the presents.

Christmas Day is for church, family, and feasting. Pasta dishes and turkey are served. *Panettone,* a Christmas cake filled with raisins, citron, and other fruits, is eaten at the end of the meal. There might also be *panaforte* (strong bread) and *cassata* (ice cream and fruit trifle). *Pizelles* are popular molded cookies made with a special baking iron. Macaroons are also popular.

New Year's Day is a day of merry parties and friends. It is also the day for adults to exchange gifts. This includes community workers. For example, a police officer directing traffic may find gifts handed to him from passing motorists.

Children traditionally wait until Epiphany (January 6) to receive their gifts from La Befana. Legend describes Befana as a tiny old woman dressed in black and riding a broomstick from house to house on the Eve of Epiphany. Sometimes she uses her broomstick to slide down chimneys, and other times she comes through a window. But she always leaves gifts in the shoes of good children, a piece of firewood for the poor, and lumps of coal or bags of ashes for the bad children. (She may even take the really wicked children with her!)

Befana travels in search of the Christ Child. The story says that she was busy sweeping when the Three Kings came searching for Jesus. They stopped at Befana's house and asked her to go along, but she refused because she had so much work to do. She said she would join them when she finished, and they went on without her. After she finished cleaning, she gathered some gifts and set out to find them, but instead she got lost. She is still searching for him today and leaves a gift in every child's home on Epiphany Eve.

ACTIVITIES

1. Read the story of Befana to your students. A version is found in *An American Christmas* (Allied Books Ltd.)

2. Use the patterns on pages 44-45 to make flannel board figures to tell the story of Befana to the students. You can also let the students use the patterns to make puppet figures. They can practice telling Befana's story, and then they can share it with another class.

3. Discuss what lesson Befana learned. (For example, we must grasp joy and celebration when we have the opportunity, or we may lose that chance forever). Encourage students to remember and share personal experiences they have had and the lessons they have learned. Then write new "folk tales" to illustrate one or more of these lessons.

4. What does Befana look like? After reading the legend of Befana, let the students illustrate their interpretation of her. Share and compare. Is she mean? Is she kindly? How is she dressed?

5. Make a *presepio*. Follow the directions below to create a special silhouette image.

6. Follow the recipes on page 46 to make macaroons and biscotti.

7. Sing the Italian Christmas carols found on page 47.

PRESEPIO SILHOUETTE

Materials:

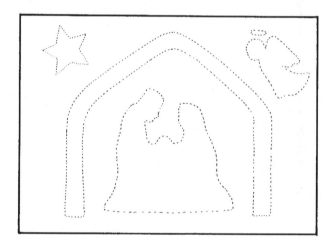

- patterns (page 43)
- 9" x 12" (22.5 cm x 30 cm) black and blue construction paper
- 2" (5 cm) square yellow construction paper or gold foil
- 2" x 2¹/₂" (5 cm x 6.25 cm) white construction paper
- scissors
- pencil
- white crayon
- rubber cement (or paper paste)

Directions:

1. Place the whole pattern page on top of black construction paper and press hard while tracing around the outlines of the patterns. This should leave an imprint on the black paper. If necessary, trace along this imprint with a white crayon.

2. Carefully poke the scissor point through the center of each figure and cut out along the imprinted lines. Trim as needed to leave smooth openings. Remove and discard each figure. Leave the black paper outlines intact.*

3. Place the yellow paper underneath the star opening, trim off any excess, and glue to the back of the black paper around the edges.

4. Place the white paper underneath the angel opening, trim off any excess, and glue to the back of the black paper around the edges.

5. Place the entire black paper on top of the blue background paper, keeping the star and angel areas clear. Glue around all edges.

6. Let dry and hang in a window.

   *****(*Note: Younger students can cut out the figure patterns from black, yellow, and white paper, and then glue them to a blue background. Frame with 1" (2.5 cm) border of black.*)

PRESEPIO SILHOUETTE PATTERN
See page 42 for directions.

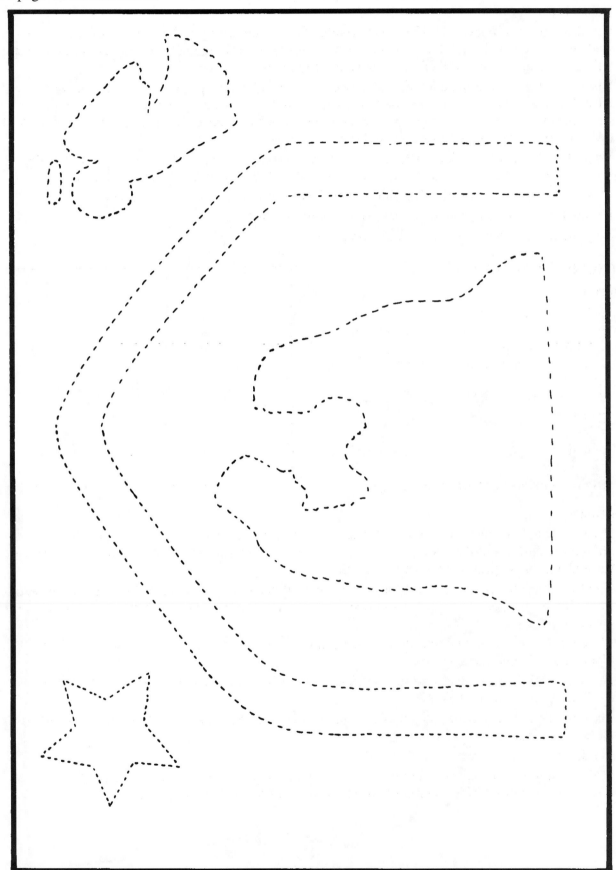

BEFANA PATTERNS
See page 42 for directions.

BEFANA PATTERNS *(cont.)*

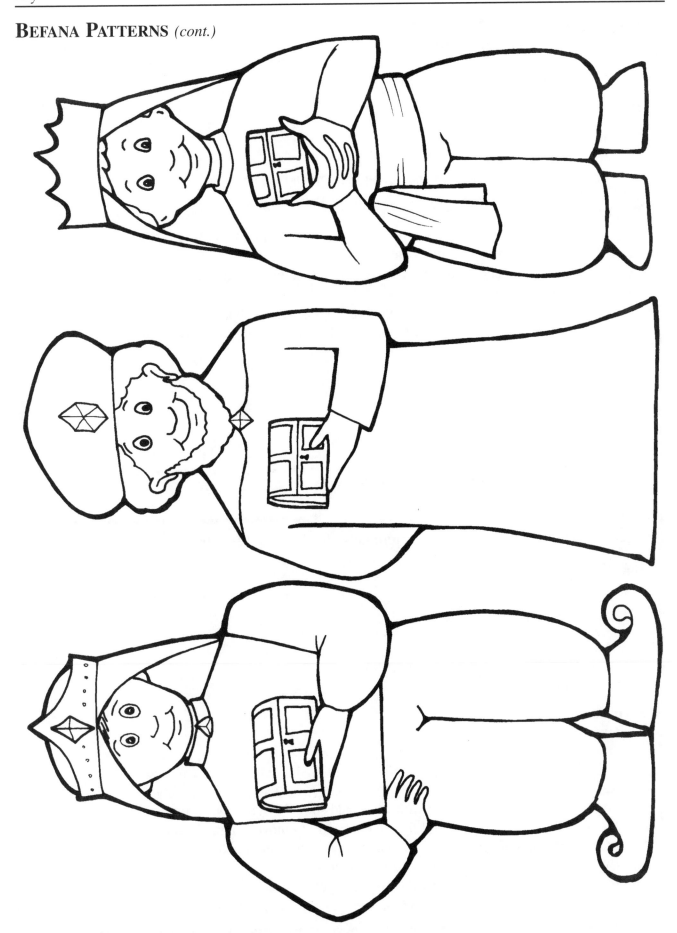

Macaroons

These cookies are a delicious Italian Christmas treat.

Ingredients:

- 4 egg whites
- ¹/₂ t. (2.5 mL) salt
- 2 c. (500 mL) sugar
- ¹/₂ c. (125 mL) blanched almonds, finely ground in blender
- 1 t. (5 mL) almond extract

Preparation:

1. Preheat oven to 350° F (180° C). Line cookie sheets with unglazed brown paper.
2. Beat egg whites and salt until creamy.
3. Add the sugar about ¹/₄ cup (65 mL) at a time. Beat until peaks are stiff.
4. Fold in the almonds and extract.
5. Drop by tablespoonfuls onto the lined cookie sheet. Bake about 10–15 minutes until light brown and dry in appearance. Let cool slightly, then remove from the paper.

Biscotti

Biscotti are twice-baked crisp cookies from Italy. Recipe will make about 1¹/₂ dozen.

Ingredients:

- ¹/₄ c. (65 mL) butter
- ¹/₂ c. (125 mL) sugar
- 1¹/₄ t. (6.25 mL) baking powder
- 1 t. (5 mL) shredded orange peel
- ¹/₄ c. (65 mL) chopped mixed candied fruit
- ¹/₈ t. (.6 mL) anise extract

- 1¹/₂ c. (375 mL) flour
- 1 egg
- ¹/₄ c. (65 mL) candied red cherries
- water
- sugar

Preparation:

1. Preheat oven to 375° F (190° C).
2. Beat butter until softened. Beat in ¹/₂ c. (125 mL) flour. Add sugar, egg, baking powder, and anise flavoring. Beat thoroughly. Mix in remaining ingredients until well blended.
3. Shape dough into an 11" x 2" x 1" (27.5 cm x 5 cm x 2.5 cm) loaf and place on an ungreased cookie sheet. Brush with water and sprinkle lightly with sugar.
4. Bake for 20–25 minutes or until lightly browned. Remove from the oven and cool for 1 hour. Turn oven off. When the loaf is cool, preheat oven to 325° F (170° C) and proceed.
5. Cut the loaf diagonally into ¹/₂" (1.25 cm) thick slices.
6. Place slices, cut side down, on an ungreased cookie sheet.
7. Bake for 10–15 minutes or until dry and crisp. Remove from the cookie sheet and cool.

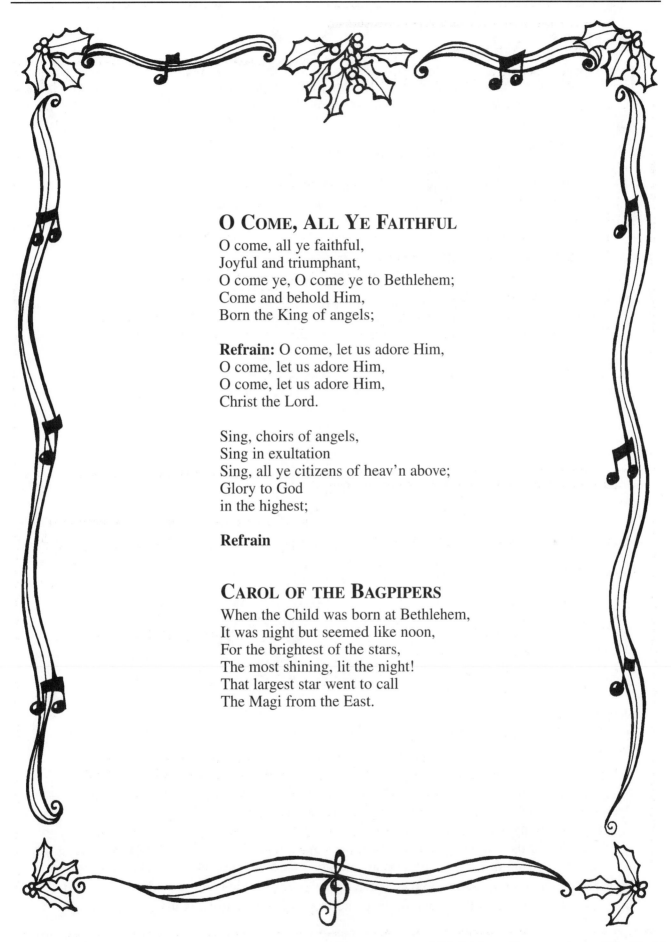

O Come, All Ye Faithful

O come, all ye faithful,
Joyful and triumphant,
O come ye, O come ye to Bethlehem;
Come and behold Him,
Born the King of angels;

Refrain: O come, let us adore Him,
O come, let us adore Him,
O come, let us adore Him,
Christ the Lord.

Sing, choirs of angels,
Sing in exultation
Sing, all ye citizens of heav'n above;
Glory to God
in the highest;

Refrain

Carol of the Bagpipers

When the Child was born at Bethlehem,
It was night but seemed like noon,
For the brightest of the stars,
The most shining, lit the night!
That largest star went to call
The Magi from the East.

Japan

Most Japanese people are not Christians, so the religious aspects of the holiday usually take place in churches and schools run by foreign missionaries. There, Christmas is a time to share the Christmas message through elaborate programs and worship services. But Christmas is also enjoyed by non-Christians in a secular fashion. The Japanese greeting is *"Meri Kurisumasu!"*

In the past few decades, Japan has adopted many western Christmas practices, such as the exchanging of gifts, the eating of roast turkey, and caroling. The Japanese also enjoy decorating store windows and homes with such things as paper holly, mistletoe, and bells. Christmas trees are adorned with tiny fans, lanterns, flowers, and dolls. In some places, Santa Claus is said to visit the children, but the unique gift bearer to the Japanese is *Hoteiosho.* He is a Japanese god who travels on foot. He has eyes in the front and back of his head to observe the behavior of the children. To the good children he gives a toy from the bag he carries on his back.

New Year's Day is really the biggest celebration for Japan. This resembles the Christmas celebrations of much of the western world. Special ceremonies, visiting with family and friends, music, kites, and sparkling homes are all included in this holiday.

ACTIVITIES

1. Describe Hoteiosho and ask the students to write a story about what he sees on his travels around Japan. Then ask them to draw a picture of him. Display the stories and illustrations.
2. Make a Japanese fan. Follow the directions below.

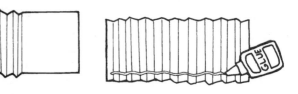

FOLDED FAN

Materials:

- two 4¹/₂" x 12" (11.5 cm x 30 cm) pieces of Christmas wrapping paper
- rubber cement or slightly thinned white glue
- paper clip
- 15" (37.5 cm) ribbon
- ruler and pencil

Directions:

1. Glue the wrapping paper pieces together, right sides out. Press under a heavy book until dry.
2. Trim off any uneven edges.
3. With a ruler, measure and mark a line ¹/₂" (1.25 cm) from the short edge. This is your guide.
4. Fold back and forth on the guide line, accordion style, the entire length of paper. Crease well.
5. Open the fan and place a line of glue along one long edge. Fold the fan again and hold the glued edge together with a paper clip. Let it dry. Remove the paper clip.
6. Spread the top of the fan open and bend the lower outer edges into two triangles to help prop the fan in an open position. Add a drop of glue and press each edge together to hold. Let dry.
7. Tie the ribbon into an attractive bow and attach it with glue to the base of the fan.
8. **Optional:** Add a yarn or string loop to the center back of the fan to hang it from the tree.

Mexico

At Christmastime in Mexico, you might be greeted with "Feliz Navidad!" In Mexico, there are many special Christmas traditions. The majority of Mexicans are Roman Catholic, so religious elements are important to their celebrations.

Las Posadas (the processions) is the most important Christmas custom for Mexicans. It is a ritual beginning on December 16 and continuing for eight more nights until Christmas Eve. (This is the amount of time it took Mary and Joseph to travel to Bethlehem.) Families and friends participate in a procession to search for shelter each night, just like the Holy Family did on the night of Jesus' birth. The people divide into two groups: the innkeepers and the travelers. Houses are chosen ahead of time, and one is designated to be the final inn. The first people in the group of travelers carry statues of Mary and Joseph. All the others carry candles. They sing and ask for lodging as they walk from house to house, but the innkeepers always answer, "No. There is no room in the inn." Finally, the last innkeeper recognizes the holy couple and says, "Yes, I can offer you lodging." At this point, the whole group enters, eats, and celebrates. On Christmas Eve, the final night of Las Posadas, a figure of the Baby Jesus is carefully placed in the manger scene at the final stop before the celebration begins.

This celebration is especially enjoyed by the children. In addition to special foods like buñuelos (fried sugar tortillas) and Mexican hot chocolate, there is a decorated piñata hanging from the ceiling. Blindfolded children take turns trying to break it open with a stick. When it finally breaks, candy and gifts from the piñata's heart fall out, and the children rush to gather them. The traditional piñatas are made in animal or star shapes of terra-cotta (clay) and covered with colored paper. Many of today's piñatas are made of papier-mâché.

Pastorelas are another custom in many areas of Mexico. They are plays that vary in length, but each shows the shepherds' journey to the scene of the nativity. They also contain some elements of Mexican and Indian folklore.

Paper lanterns called *farolitos* are another Mexican tradition. These have become popular in many areas of the western world today and are often called *luminarias*. Mexicans place candles in brown paper bags which have been carefully cut to cast special shadows. They set these out along sidewalks, streets, rooftops, and window sills to light the way for the processions.

After nine evenings of processions and celebrations, Christmas Day is a quiet time. Families go to church and get together to eat things like oxtail soup, turkey, fruits, *empanaditas* (little meat pies), *enchiladas* (cheese and/or meat and sauce-filled tortillas), *flan* (custard pudding), and cake.

Children usually have to wait until January 6 to receive their gifts from the Three Kings. They leave their shoes on the window sills and await the Twelfth Night visit. However, as American influence spreads, many children also receive gifts from Santa Claus on Christmas Eve.

The most famous Christmas "flower" originated in Mexico. The red- and green-leafed poinsettia grows wild in damp ravines and ditches throughout the country. In 1829, the U.S. ambassador to Mexico came back to the United States with several plants, and they became very popular. There is a legend about the plant's link to Christmas. A poor Mexican child wanted to give a gift to the Virgin Mary, but he had nothing to give. The child picked some weeds and laid them at the foot of the statue. Miraculously, they turned into beautiful, star-shaped flowers with the color of fire and light.

ACTIVITIES

1. Read the legend of the poinsettia to your students. A version is retold by Pamela Kennedy in *A Child's Book of Christmas*.

2. Let your students write their own poinsettia legends explaining how they think the flower came to be.

3. Make farolitos. Directions can be found below.

4. Make poinsettias. Use the patterns on page 51 to construct the flowers and leaves. Trace or duplicate the petals onto red paper and the leaves onto green. Glue small yellow circles in the center.

5. Perform the story of Las Posadas using the traditional script found on page 52. As a group, create illustrations on mural paper, include the dialogue, and display the mural in the hallway.

6. Try the traditional Mexican Christmas carol on page 54. It is often sung by children on Christmas Eve in anticipation of the breaking of the piñata. The carol is given in both Spanish and English.

7. Follow the recipes on page 53 to make Ensalada de Noche Buena and Mexican hot chocolate.

8. Using balloons, newspapers, and thinned glue, make your own piñatas.

FAROLITO

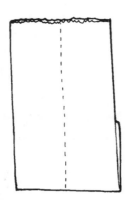

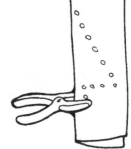

Materials:

- paper lunch bag
- hole punch
- pencil
- sand
- votive candle

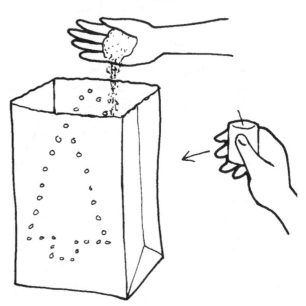

Directions:

1. Choose a simple pattern shape where both sides of the pattern are the same (e.g., a simple Christmas tree or evergreen wreath).

2. Fold the bag in half lengthwise. Draw half of the pattern shape on the front of the paper bag against the fold. (See illustration.)

3. Using the hole punch, make evenly spaced holes along the design line.

4. Unfold and open the bag. Place some sand in the bottom and set the votive candle inside.

5. Set several farolitos in a row. Light the candles carefully for a beautiful display of lights and shadows. (Note: Paper bags are, of course, highly flammable. Use both discretion and caution.)

POINSETTIA PATTERNS

See page 50 for directions.

LAS POSADAS

Travelers: Who will give shelter to these travelers who sing of walking the roads?

Innkeeper #1: Even though you say you are worn out, we do not give shelter to those we do not know.

Joseph: In heaven's name, I ask for shelter since my beloved wife cannot walk any further.

Innkeeper #2: Here there is no room, so keep on walking. I cannot open up for just anyone passing by.

Chorus: Do not be inhumane; have a heart. God will reward you.

Innkeeper #3: Better leave now and stop bothering me. If you anger me, I will chase you away.

Joseph: Weary and worn, we go on our way,
Lodging to seek wherever we may;
A carpenter from Nazareth I am,
Journeying afar to Bethlehem.
Mary, my loved one, needs shelter tonight—
We beg you to help us, in our sad plight.

Travelers: He asks for shelter, beloved innkeeper, for only one night, for the Queen of Heaven.

Joseph: My wife is Mary, the Queen of Heaven, who soon will become mother of Christ by the word of God.

Innkeeper #4: *(To Mary and Joseph)* Is it you, Joseph? And your wife, Mary? Come in, wanderers. I did not recognize you. We will give you shelter with great joy. Come in, good Joseph, come in with Mary!
(To the rest of the group) Come in, holy wanderers; receive our good favor. There is nothing in this poor dwelling but our hearts.

Travelers: This is a joyful night of pleasure and rejoicing because here we give shelter to the Mother of the Son of God!

Ensalada de Noche Buena

This special "Christmas Eve Salad" is a Mexican delight.

Ingredients:
- 20 oz. (600 g) can pineapple chunks (drained)
- 2 oranges (peeled and sectioned)
- 2 bananas (peeled and sliced)
- 1 apple (cored and sliced into wedges)
- 2 T. (30 mL) orange or lemon juice
- lettuce leaves
- ¹/₂ c. (125 mL) peanuts
- ¹/₄ c. (65 mL) salad dressing thinned with 2 T. (30 mL) milk (optional)

Preparation:
1. Dip sliced bananas and apple wedges into orange juice.
2. Line a platter with several crisp lettuce leaves.
3. Arrange fruits in groups on the platter in an attractive manner.
4. Sprinkle on peanuts.
5. Drizzle salad dressing over fruit or pass the dressing in a separate container.

Mexican Hot Chocolate

The travellers in Las Posadas might enjoy this delicious hot chocolate drink when they reach the final "inn."

Ingredients:
- 6 c. (1.5 L) milk
- 1 c. (250 mL) semi-sweet chocolate chips
- 3 cinnamon sticks
- ¹/₂ t. (2.5 mL) ground cinnamon
- 1¹/₂ t. (7.5 mL) vanilla
- 2 T. (30 mL) sugar
- whipped cream (optional)

Preparation:
1. Heat 1 c. (250 mL) milk and chocolate chips in a large saucepan over low heat until the chocolate is melted.
2. Gradually stir in the remaining milk. Add cinnamon sticks, ground cinnamon, vanilla, and sugar, and continue to heat until the milk is almost boiling.
3. Remove the cinnamon sticks, split them in half, and place in mugs if desired.
4. Use a rotary beater and whip the milk mixture until frothy.
5. Pour into mugs and add a dollop of whipped cream, if desired.

EL CANCION DE LA PIÑATA (*Spanish*)

En las noches de posadas
La piñata es lo mejor;
La niña mas remilgada
Se alborata con ardor.
Dale, dale, dale!
No pierdas el ti no quede la
Distancia se pierde el camino

THE PIÑATA SONG (*English*)

On the nights of the posadas
The piñata is the best;
The shyest little girl
Bursts forth with joy.
Hit it, hit it, hit it!
Don't lose the aim
That gives the distance.

NOCHE DE PAZ (*Spanish*)*

Noche de paz,
Noche de amor,
Todo duerme en derredor.
Entre los astros que esparcen su luz.
Bella anunciando al niñito Jesus.
Brilla la estrella de paz.
Brilla la estrella de paz.

Noche de paz,
Noche de amor,
Ved que bello resplandor.
Luce en el rostro del niño Jesus.
En el pesebre, del mundo la luz.
Astro de eterno fulgor.
Astro de eterno fulgor.

*The English version, "Silent Night,"
can be found on page 12.*

Netherlands

*Z*alig Kerstfeest and *Hartelijke Kerst Groeten* are Dutch Christmas greetings. *Sinter Klaas*, now *Santa Claus* in the United States, is the Dutch gift bearer, and gift giving, delicious desserts, and festive windmills are all important parts of Christmas in the Netherlands.

Sinter Klaas is the Dutch name for Saint Nicholas. He may arrive in the Netherlands as early as November to prepare for the night of delivering gifts to the good children of the country. He has a white beard, white hair, a tall red headdress, and long robes, and he carries a tall golden staff much like a shepherd's crook. He brings along his white horse and his servant, Zwarte Piet (Black Peter). *Zwarte Piet* carries a big red book which lists the names of those children who have been naughty. He also carries a bag full of fruits, chocolates, special Dutch cookies, small gifts, and birchtree switches. Of course, the good children will get the nice treats and the naughty children will receive the switches.

On December 5, Sinter Klaas Eve, children set their wooden shoes by the fireplace, window, or kitchen stove. They fill them with hay or carrots for the white horse, and they await Sinter Klaas' arrival. Zwarte Piet descends the chimney to exchange gifts for the hay and carrots.

Other gift giving also takes place at this time or on Christmas Eve. The Dutch like surprises! It is the custom to wrap each small gift very carefully and perhaps disguise its shape or size in order to surprise the recipient. There may be many different layers of paper to unwrap before finding the gift. Each gift also holds a poem or rhyme that is intended to be funny. "Fast poets" called *sneldichters* often work in stores during the Christmas season to write and sell these verses. But, of course, the verses will be signed by Sinter Klaas or Zwarte Piet.

The Christmas season is announced on the first Sunday of Advent with the blowing of horns. The horns are made from hollow elder tree branches, and the sound travels from house to house.

Holland celebrates Christmas on December 25 and 26. Gift-giving has passed, so these two days are spent at church services, family dinners, and musical concerts. The noon meal on Christmas Day is called *Koffietafel* and resembles a huge breakfast. At seven o'clock, families enjoy a ham meal with other traditional favorites.

ACTIVITIES

1. Become a sneldichter! In small groups or individually, write short poems or rhymes to be attached to gifts. They should be humorous and written with the recipient in mind. Start with two or four short lines. They do not have to rhyme. They should be "signed" by either Sinter Klaas or Zwarte Piet. To get students started, share with them the following example written for a child who has a little trouble keeping a clean room:

   Where did you leave your wooden shoe
   For Sinter Klass to find?
   If you left it in your room,
   Too bad—there will be no gifts for you.
   (He cannot see the shoe!)
   —from Zwarte Piet

2. Make a pinwheel ornament to represent the windmills for which Holland is famous. Directions are on page 56.

3. Make "wooden" shoes. Follow the directions on page 56.

4. A recipe for the traditional *letterbanket* can be found on page 57.

5. Read the traditional Christmas song, "Hear How the Wind Blows" (page 58). Then, look up some facts about the Netherlands' weather to determine why this is meaningful for the people.

PINWHEEL ORNAMENT

Materials:

- construction paper (red, green, blue, and white)
- rubber cement or other good paper glue
- scissors
- small paper fasteners
- ruler
- pencil
- nickel (or similar round "pattern")

Directions:

1. **Teacher:** Cut the construction paper into 4¹/₂" (11 cm) squares. Each student will need two squares of contrasting colors.
2. **Students:** Choose any two colors of squares. Glue them together, matching all edges.
3. Use your ruler to draw a straight diagonal line from one corner to the other. Repeat with the other two corners, as illustrated.
4. Place the nickel in the middle of the square where the lines intersect. Trace around it.
5. Carefully cut along the drawn lines, stopping at the outer edge of the traced circle.
6. As illustrated, fold the points in sequence, overlapping them slightly at the center.
7. Poke a small hole in the center through all points and push a paper fastener through. Secure the corners down by opening the fastener on the back side.
8. Use a paper punch or needle to make a small hole in the top. Attach an ornament hook or piece of yarn to make a hanger. Hang it on your Christmas tree.

   Option: To make a toy pinwheel gift for a child, laminate the pieces before folding. Attach a straw or craft stick to the backside for a handle. Be sure that the paper fastener is a little loose so that the pinwheel can spin freely.

"WOODEN" SHOE

Materials:

- 2 c. (500 mL) sawdust
- 1¹/₂ c. (375 mL) flour
- waxed paper
- 1 c. (250 mL) salt
- ²/₃ c. (170 mL) water (approximate)

Directions:

(To make a 8" (20 cm) shoe, each student will need to mix a full batch of dough. To make smaller ones, several students can share one batch.

1. Display some pictures of wooden shoes for reference.
2. Mix the dry ingredients together in a bowl.
3. Stir in water, a little at a time, and work it together with your hands until you can form a ball.
4. Shape the dough into a wooden shoe. Be sure the shoe will stand flat and has an opening for treats. (Crumple a piece of waxed paper and put it inside, if necessary, to prop the shoe open.)
5. Set the shoe on waxed paper and let it dry 5–7 days.
6. If desired, paint the shoe using Dutch designs.
7. On December 5, set the shoes out for Sinter Klaas to fill!

Letterbanket

Letterbanket (Dutch letters) are formed from this dough for holiday treats. Wreaths with green frosting, called kerstkrans, may also be formed.

Ingredients:

- ¹/₂ lb. (225 g) butter or margarine
- 2 c. (500 mL) flour
- a pinch salt
- ¹/₂ c. (125 mL) ice water
- water

- 8 oz. (225 g) almond paste
- 1 c. (250 mL) sugar
- 1 egg (slightly beaten)
- ¹/₂ t. (2.5 mL) vanilla
- 2 t. (10 mL) sugar

Preparation for Dough:

1. Cut butter into small pieces. Use a pastry blender or two knives to mix well with flour. It will look like coarse meal.
2. Stir in ice water and mix well. The dough will be soft. Refrigerate overnight to make the dough very stiff.

Preparation for Filling:

1. Break up the almond paste into tiny pieces with a fork, your hands, or a grater.
2. With your hands, work in the sugar and vanilla.
3. Add the egg and stir with a fork until well blended.
4. Shape small quantities into sausage-like rolls. Each roll should be about ³/₄" (2 cm) in diameter and 4" (10 cm) long.
5. Roll the shapes in waxed paper and refrigerate several hours until stiff.

Letterbanket *(cont.)*

Preparation for Letterbanket:

1. Lightly flour a work surface and rolling pin. Preheat oven to 400° F (200° C). Sprinkle flour on the cookie sheet.
2. Divide the dough into 4 parts. Shape each part into a long, even roll with a flat top.
3. With the rolling pin, flatten each piece of dough on the floured board into a long rectangle shape about 4" (10 cm) wide and ¹/₈" (.3 cm) thick. Each rectangle will be 10–12" (25–30 cm) long. DO NOT roll dough too thin!
4. Place a portion of the filling along the length of the dough to within 1" (2.5 cm) of the ends.
5. Lap the dough over the almond mixture, pinch closed, and seal the ends with a little water so the filling will not run out.
6. Place the seam side down on the floured cookie sheet. Shape the roll into the initial of the person to whom this treat will be given (or shape it into a wreath).
7. Brush the tops with water and sprinkle each with ¹/₂ t. (2.5 mL) sugar.
8. Bake at 400° F (200° C) for about 30 minutes. Do not overbake. Cool.
9. You may wish to frost any wreaths with green icing.

HEAR HOW THE WIND BLOWS

Hear how the wind blows through the trees,
It whistles within the house!
Will the good saint come to visit
With weather so foul?
Yes, he'll come in the dark of night,
Riding his fast-paced horse!
He'll surely come
If he knows we are waiting,
Yes, he'll surely come.
Yes, then, he'll surely come,
Listen, children. Who knocks at the door?
Listen, children. Who taps softly at the window?
Surely it is a stranger,
Who is surely lost and cold.
Come, let us ask his name.
Saint Nicholas,
Saint Nicholas,
Come visit us tonight.
We've put straw and goodies in every corner.

Nigeria

Since nearly 40 percent of Nigerians are Christians, Christmas is a holiday anticipated with joy. As a Christmas greeting there, you might hear "Merry Christmas," but more likely it will be a hearty *"Yesu yana Kaunacce ni"* (Jesus loves me).

Big church programs and pageants are considered key for spreading the gospel to non-Christians. Christmas plays are elaborate and lengthy. Gift-giving is not widely practiced in Nigeria, but on Christmas Day families often exchange food. They make extra quantities of chicken stew, rice, and other foods, and they send portions to their neighbors.

Music is very important to the people of Nigeria. On Christmas afternoon, children go from house to house singing carols and hoping for candies and cookies. Some children wear decorative masks. Drums are considered the most important musical instrument, and they are used along with other rhythm instruments to enhance the pageants, to accompany singing, and to announce the Savior's birth.

ACTIVITIES

1. Make a drum to celebrate the holiday with music. See the directions below.
2. Make a decorative holiday mask or mask ornament. Follow the directions on page 60.

DRUM

Materials:

- empty oatmeal, coffee, or plastic container with lid
- construction paper or heavy bond paper
- scissors
- tape or glue
- pencils or dowels
- cotton balls
- canvas or burlap
- string
- rubber bands

Directions:

1. Choose a container for the drum. Wrap the sides with construction paper and trim it to fit. Tape or glue the edges to the container.
2. Measure and cut a piece of canvas or burlap at least 2" (5 cm) larger than the circumference of the lid. Place the lid on the container and stretch the canvas over the top. Tie string tightly around the top to hold the canvas on the drum. Add glue if necessary for reinforcement.
3. To make the drumsticks, tape two or three cotton balls to one end of a pencil or dowel rod. Cover with canvas or burlap, and secure with a rubber band. Trim off excess fabric.

(**Note:** To decorate the drum, do the following before or just after covering the drum with construction paper. Dip pieces of yarn, string, or rope into a glue and water mixture. Pull the yarn through your fingers to remove extra glue, and make interesting designs with the yarn on blocks of wood, squares of poster board, or cardboard rolls. Let the design dry. Then dip the yarn surface into tempera paint and roll or stamp the print onto the construction paper.)

MASK

Materials:

- paper plate
- pencil
- scissors
- large craft stick, paint stirrer, or tongue depressor
- tempera paints, markers, puff paints, etc.
- pictures of African masks

Optional Materials:

- glue
- feathers
- straw
- yarn
- beads
- raffia
- glitter

Directions:

1. Place a paper plate against your face and mark the place for your eyes, nose, and mouth with a pencil. (You may need a friend for help.)
2. Cut out holes for eyes, nose, and mouth.
3. Decorate the mask. Use the pictures for ideas to stimulate your own creativity.
4. Tape the craft stick to the base of the mask as a handle. Hold the mask to cover your face as you sing Christmas carols or go caroling through the school.

Variation:

Make a mask ornament to hang on a Christmas tree by cutting a 4" (10 cm) oval from poster board and decorating it as directed above. Omit the craft stick, but apply a yarn or thread hanging loop to the back instead.

Philippines

Christmas celebrations in the Philippines are a mixture of Chinese, Spanish, European, and American customs. The main Christmas symbol is the Christmas star. It is found everywhere, hanging in windows, lighted like a lantern, and carried in parades. The "Parade of the Stars" takes place on Christmas Eve. Large stars, sometimes reaching 30 feet (9 m) across, are elaborately decorated and carried, and prizes are given to the most beautiful stars.

The holiday begins on December 16 with the sounds of bells, firecrackers, and bamboo cannons. Roosters add to the noise at the 4 A.M. church service, *The Mass of Cocks*. Christmas Eve includes a midnight mass. When the Bible story is read, a star glides down a wire from the choirloft and lands appropriately in the Nativity scene. After church, people visit little stalls for coffee, tea, and fruit juices. On Christmas Day, families and friends visit and exchange gifts. Parties and gift-giving continue until January 6, Three Kings Day.

ACTIVITY

Make a Christmas star. Directions follow.

FILIPINO CHRISTMAS STAR

Materials:

- ten 2" (5 cm) pieces pipe cleaner
- 5 plastic drinking straws
- white glue
- two 10" (25 cm) squares regular or metallic tissue paper
- five 1" (2.5 cm) pieces pipe cleaner
- waxed paper
- five 12" (30 cm) squares tissue paper

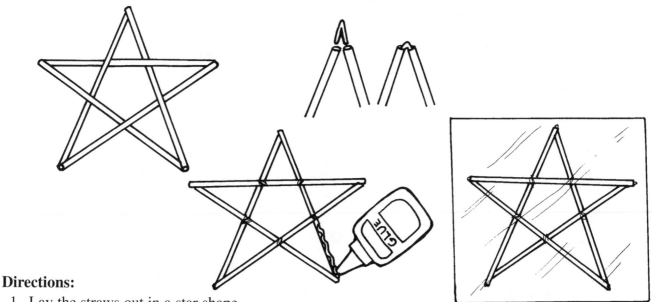

Directions:

1. Lay the straws out in a star shape.
2. Bend five 2" (5 cm) pieces of pipe cleaner in half and insert each end into the end of two straws to hold the straws together (making a star point). Add a drop of glue to each point if needed to stabilize the star shape.
3. Adjust the star shape so it is even. Using the five remaining 2" (5 cm) pieces of pipe cleaner, fasten the inside of the star together by bending each one around two intersecting straws.
4. Place the star shape on waxed paper. Apply a bead of glue along the straws, points, and intersections.
5. Place one 10" (25cm) piece of tissue paper on top of the glue. Press lightly and let it dry for five minutes.

FILIPINO CHRISTMAS STAR *(cont.)*

6. Carefully turn the star and tissue paper over. Repeat with glue on this side and place the other 10" (25 cm) piece of tissue on top. Let it dry for at least one hour.

7. When dry, use scissors to trim off excess tissue paper around the star frame, allowing at least a ½" (1.25 cm) border.

8. Fold each 12" (30 cm) square of tissue paper into thirds. You will now have five 12" x 4" (30 cm x 10 cm) strips.

9. Clip the strips at ½" (1.25 cm) intervals to within 1" (2.5 cm) of the top edge.

10. Place the 1" (2.5 cm) pipe cleaners at one end of each strip, with about half of each protruding above the strip. Add a drop of glue.

11. Begin rolling the strip tightly around the pipe cleaner. Add glue as needed.

12. When you reach the end of the strip, add a drop of glue and squeeze the tissue around the pipe cleaner so the fringed area flares out.

13. Insert each protruding end of pipe cleaner into one straw end at each star point. Let it dry well.

14. Add a piece of yarn or string to the star to hang it up. The star looks lovely in a window or other area where light can shine through it.

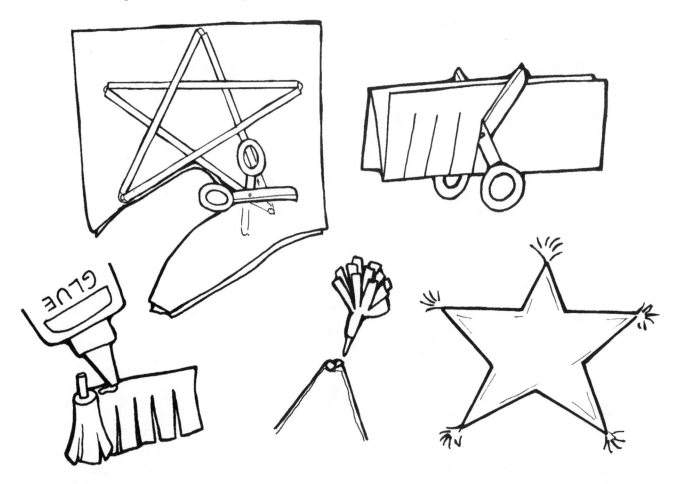

Ornament Variation:

Follow the same instructions as above but use smaller pieces of straw and tissue paper. Cut the straws in half, cut the tissue to 6" (15 cm), but leave the pipe cleaners the same sizes as above for easy handling.

Poland

*B*oze Narodzenie! Wesolych Swiat! These are the Christmas greetings in Poland. Christmas is a joyous time for the Polish people. Children in Poland receive two sets of gifts. St. Nicholas leaves large gifts, apples, and heart-shaped honey spice cakes on December 6. On Christmas Eve, the Star Man leaves smaller but equally important gifts from the stars and the Wise Men.

Stars are the most important Christmas symbol in Poland. The Polish celebration of Christmas begins in earnest when the first star is seen on Christmas Eve. It is a solemn occasion. Families share *oplatek* (small bread-like wafers) to end fasting, and then they eat a festive meal. At one time, twelve different foods were served to represent the twelve apostles (Jesus' twelve followers during his adult ministries). These foods included soups, fish, noodles, dumplings, fruits, cookies, and cakes. Today, a compote including twelve different fruits is more common.

The Christmas Eve table is set with a white tablecloth, and straw is scattered underneath the table as a reminder of Christ's birth in a stable. There is an extra place set at the table for the Christ Child or an unexpected guest. The house is considered blessed if a hungry person fills that spot. Leftovers from the meal are fed to the animals who are believed to speak on this special evening.

Earlier on Christmas Eve, children write a letter to Mother Star or the Three Wise Men and leave it on a window sill. After the meal, the Star Man visits. (He is often a disguised neighbor or priest.) He may be accompanied by helpers called Star Boys and other children dressed in animal costumes. Star Man asks the children questions about their Bible lessons. If they answer correctly, they are rewarded with small presents. If not, Star Man scolds them. They all join in singing carols.

Families go to a midnight mass called *Pasterka.* Christmas Day is spent visiting friends and relatives. There is no cooking on this day. Homes are decorated with sheaves of grain and a fir tree. The trees always hold stars as well as birds, angels, colored paper and ribbons, and *pajaki,* which resembles a spider's web. In the week between Christmas and New Year's Day, the Christmas story is reenacted many times using puppets and a manger scene called a *Joselki.* Today's puppet shows also include secular scenes. Celebrations continue until Epiphany when Star Man returns for one last visit.

ACTIVITIES

1. Read "In Clean Hay" by Eric P. Kelly, found in *An American Christmas* (Allied Books Ltd.)
2. Make an angel ornament. Directions are below and on page 64.
3. Make twelve-fruit compote. The recipe is on page 64.

FOLDED ANGEL ORNAMENT

Materials:

- 1" (2.5 cm) styrofoam ball
- stapler
- white glue
- 1 sheet 8½" x 11" (22 cm x 28 cm) thin paper
- 3" (7.5 cm) piece metallic pipe cleaner (gold or silver)
- matching metallic/cotton cording or trim (for hanger)

Directions:

1. Cut the paper in fourths so that you have four pieces measuring 4¼" x 5½" (11 cm x 14 cm). (See illustrations next page.)
2. On the *short* edge of one piece of paper, mark a line ³/₈" (1 cm) wide.
3. Fold along the line. Continue to fold accordion-style across the entire paper. This is the body.
4. On the *long* edge of another piece of paper, mark a line ³/₈" (1 cm) wide. Fold accordion-style. This is the wings.

FOLDED ANGEL ORNAMENT (cont.)

5. Fold the wings in half lengthwise.

6. Place one end of the folded body inside the fold of the wings as illustrated and staple through all the layers.

7. Gently push the stapled edge about ⅓ of the way into the styrofoam ball.

8. Remove the ball and place some glue in the opening. Reinsert the body and wings. Let dry.

9. Bend the pipe cleaner around your finger to make a circle. Twist the end to hold it in place. Extend the remaining length down to insert the "halo" into the back of the angel's head. Adjust the halo to stand upright.

10. Fan out the wings and body. Tie a hanger to the neck or halo to hang the ornament on the tree.

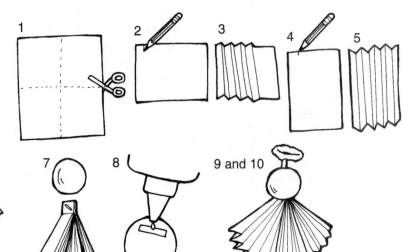

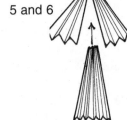

5 and 6

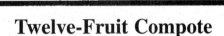

7   8   9 and 10

Twelve-Fruit Compote

Ingredients:

- 12 fruits (canned, dried, or fresh)*
- 10 oz. (300 g) current jelly
- ½ c. (125 mL) water

Preparation:

1. *With the students, list as many fruits as you can. Choose 12 of their favorites which are also readily available in your grocery store. (Some to consider include cherries, apples, pears, figs, apricots, peaches, oranges, raisins, grapes, plums, lemons, and prunes.) Purchase small amounts of these fruits.

2. Cut the fruit into small pieces. Combine them in a large bowl and mix well.

3. Mix the current jelly and water in a large saucepan. Heat until dissolved and well mixed.

4. Add the fruit and simmer on low until the fruit is tender. Serve warm in bowls.

Russia

Though in most recent years Christmas was not officially recognized in this country, Christians have always celebrated it. *"Hristos Razdajetsja!"* is their greeting.

Dyed Maroz (Grandfather Frost) is the Russian version of Santa Claus. He is dressed in a red suit and has a white beard, but he usually delivers gifts on New Year's Day. A traditional gift is a *Matryoshka* doll. The outer doll is opened to reveal smaller dolls nested inside. The other gift bearer for whom Russia is famous is an old woman called *Babouschka.* Her legend is similar to Italy's Befana. It seems Babouschka was visited by the Three Kings, but she was too busy spinning to help them find the Christ Child. Perhaps she intentionally misdirected them. Because of her error, she is doomed to wander forever, delivering gifts to good children. She creeps into the children's houses quietly, watches them as they sleep, and then leaves a gift. Babouschka typically visits on Epiphany.

Russians enjoy singing ancient carols called *Kolyadki.* Families eat a Christmas Eve supper together and gather around a decorated tree. The Russian tree is covered with apples, oranges, candy, dolls, and fabric and foil ornaments.

ACTIVITIES

1. Read the legend of Babouschka. One version is found in *Christmas Around the World.* Ask students to illustrate the story and put it together into a book to share with other classes.
2. Make *Matryoshka* dolls. Directions are below.
3. Make fabric ball ornaments. Follow the directions on page 66.
4. Make Russian honey spice cake. A recipe can be found on page 66.

MATRYOSHKA DOLLS

Materials:

- 3 empty cans of graded sizes
- construction paper
- pencil
- tape or glue
- markers

Optional Materials:

- fabric pieces
- puff paints
- glitter

Directions:

1. Cover each tin can with a piece of plain construction paper. Tape or glue it in place.
2. Place the cans with the open end down. On each can, use a pencil to design a different person, animal, or Christmas object. It is best if all three characters are somehow related.
3. Use markers, fabrics, or other materials to fill in all the details. Be sure the designs are not too thick. Each can must fit inside the next larger can.
4. Let the cans dry, and then place the larger ones over the smaller ones.
5. Extension: Try telling a story using the three characters.

FABRIC BALL ORNAMENT

Materials:

- fabric scraps
- small styrofoam ball
- white craft glue
- 6" (15 cm) ribbon
- straight pin
- pencil or table knife

Directions:

1. Choose and cut several small fabric scraps to fit around the ball.
2. Place one piece of fabric on the ball. Use the edge of the knife or the point of the pencil to gently push the fabric edges about ⅛" (.3 cm) into the ball. Repeat with other fabric scraps.
3. Apply some glue to hold each section, if necessary.
4. When the entire ball is covered with fabric, loop the ribbon and use a straight pin to attach it to the top of the ball. Hang and enjoy.

Kovrizhka Medovaya

This honey spice cake is a Russian Christmas favorite.

Ingredients:

- 2 eggs
- 2 c. (500 mL) flour
- 1 c. (250 mL) honey
- ½ c. (125 mL) sliced almonds or other nuts
- ½ c. (125 mL) brown sugar
- ½ t. (2.5 mL) baking soda
- ½ c. (125 mL) raisins
- whipped cream or jam

Preparation:

1. Grease and flour a 9" x 5" (22.5 cm x 12.5 cm) loaf pan. Preheat oven to 350° F (180° C).
2. In a bowl, beat the eggs well.
3. Add brown sugar and mix thoroughly.
4. Mix the flour and baking soda in a separate bowl. Add egg and sugar mixture to the flour mixture. Stir well.
5. Add honey and stir for 8–10 minutes.
6. Stir in raisins.
7. Pour dough into a greased pan and spread evenly.
8. Sprinkle nuts evenly on the top.
9. Bake for 50–60 minutes or until a toothpick comes out clean.
10. Let cool 20 minutes. Slice and serve with whipped cream or jam.

Scandinavia

(Sweden, Norway, and Denmark)

The four countries (including Finland) and one island (Iceland) that make up Scandinavia have much in common and yet maintain distinct and special customs of their own as well. The Christmas season is important to most Scandinavians. A well-decorated Christmas tree can be found in virtually every home. Rich and bountiful foods are important because of the years of famine each country has suffered in the past. Clean homes are also an important tradition, and many hours are spent scrubbing in preparation for Christmas.

It was probably in Scandinavia that Santa received his sleigh and reindeer. Santa's horse would not make it through the deep snow in the cold climates of these northern countries! Each of these countries has a little gnome or elf who helps deliver gifts to the children. Although each is called by a different name, they have similar characteristics and are very dear to the people who live there.

Food is important to the Scandinavians, but most of their foods are whitish in color and rather bland in flavor compared to many countries. A variety of fish is always served. Scandinavians also remember to feed the birds and other animals at Christmas. They set out sheaves of grain, sometimes raised on high poles, to share their bounty with the birds. Cattle and horses are given extra food, and fishing nets and gaming traps are removed for the holidays.

SWEDEN

The term *Yule,* often used to refer to Christmas, actually comes from the Scandinavian word *Jule. God Jul* is the Swedish Christmas greeting. On December 13, the holiday begins with a special feast of Saint Lucia, the "Queen of Light." There are several legends associated with St. Lucia that have made her so important to the people of Sweden. One says she brought food to some Christians in hiding and wore candles on her head so her hands remained free to carry the food. She was later blinded and killed for doing this. Another legend describes her visit to Swedish peasants in a vision during a terrible famine. She wore a crown of fire in this vision and a miracle took place after her visit: ships arrived bearing grain and ending the famine. St. Lucia remains a symbol of hope and plenty.

In remembrance of St. Lucia, each year the oldest daughter in every family dresses in a long white gown with a red sash at her waist and wears a crown of candles and lingonberry leaves upon her head. She serves the rest of her family trays of coffee and special saffron-scented buns called *lussekattes* (cats). She sings "Santa Lucia." The sons (or other children) in the family may wear long white shirts and pointed paper hats upon their heads. These "Star Boys" escort St. Lucia as she brings food to family, friends, and perhaps the sick or elderly as well.

The Christmas tree is decorated with gilded pine cones, papier-mâché apples, gnomes, birds, snowflakes, paper flag garlands, and lights. Straw ornaments in the shapes of goats, pigs, stars, or crowns move gently from the heat of the tree lights. Underneath the tree are the gifts brought by *Jultomten.*

Jultomten is Sweden's version of Santa Claus. He is an elf with a long white beard and red tasseled cap. He rides a goat called *Julbrock.* A *tomten* is a mischievous gnome. He is not seen very often, but the Swedish people believe that warm bowls of rice pudding placed on their doorsteps will coax him to their houses on Christmas Eve. Often the father of the house will dress up like Jultomten when handing out gifts. Funny gifts called *julklappar* might be left after a secret knock on the door.

SCANDINAVIA *(cont.)*

On Christmas Eve, bells call people to church. At home before eating a large meal, they dip bread in a kettle of broth to remember the days of famine. *Lutefisk* (cod), boiled potatoes, herring, and other foods are eaten, and *Skansk gröt* or *Risgrynsgröt* (rice porridge) with a hidden almond finish the meal. It is believed that the lucky person who gets the almond will be married in the coming year.

Christmas Day is a quiet day for families and church. Candles and torches shine everywhere. December 26 is called "Second Day Christmas," and it is a time for parties and recreation. The holiday is not really over until January 13, St. Knut's Day. The tree is taken down, the candles are put out, and Christmas officially ends.

NORWAY

Glaedelig Jul is the Christmas greeting for both Norway and Denmark. The Advent calendar may have originated in Norway, and Advent is the beginning of their holiday. Large Advent wreaths hang above the dining room table in many Norwegian homes.

Decorations include sheaves of grain carefully preserved from the previous year's harvest. These are placed on public buildings as well as outside barns for the animals.

Norwegians are well known for providing large quantities of food for anyone who will eat it. Christmas foods are prepared throughout December, but the pace picks up by the last Sunday in Advent. This is known as "Dirt Sunday," and it is a time to forgo all housekeeping in favor of celebrating and baking. By December 23, "Little Christmas Eve," at least seven delicious dishes have been prepared, and the family gathers to sample everything.

Christmas trees will be trimmed with paper chains, stars, angels, garlands of Norwegian flags, and lights. Christmas Eve is the night for church, eating, and gift-giving. The meal might include lutefisk, *lefse* (a soft flat bread), flat bread, *julekake* (fruited bread), and lots of cookies. A creamy pudding called *rommogröt* contains a hidden almond, but instead of marrying in the next year, the finder gets to hand out the family's gifts after the meal.

The Norwegian elf is called a *nisse.* With long white beards and pointed red hats, the *nissen* resemble the tomten, but they are tinier. Nissen often reside in barns. They play tricks on people if all their work is not done before they start to celebrate. Norwegians leave a small bowl of rommogröt in the hayloft for the nissen so they will guard the farm animals well. The bowl is always empty in the morning, so the nissen must be real. (Who else would eat the porridge?) It is the *Julnisse* (Christmas elf) who is Santa's special companion and bears gifts secretly to Norwegian children on Christmas Eve.

There is always a lighted candle on Christmas Eve. According to custom, this candle must not burn out during the night or disaster will strike the family. The light will remain in the window until dawn as a cheerful welcome to strangers.

The days that follow Christmas may include something called *Julebukking* (Christmas fooling). People dressed in costumes go from house to house, but they cannot speak. The hosts must try to guess who they are. When the identities are discovered, a warm drink is offered. They are invited to put on costumes and join in the "fooling" at the next home. The group grows bigger as the night wears on.

By Epiphany, decorations are taken down and the family eats a small, simple meal of fish and potatoes. The only thing that remains is a three-armed candle representing the journey of the Wise Men.

SCANDINAVIA *(cont.)*

DENMARK

Many of Denmark's traditions mirror those of Sweden or Norway, but one unique thing is "Baking Day." It occurs several weeks before Christmas, and the dough for the traditional *brunekager* is made. It is a molasses spice cookie cut into stars or diamonds. *Glogg*, a special punch, is also Danish.

Christmas seals originated in Denmark. The money made from selling the seals is given to charity.

The *Julnisse* is Denmark's gift bearer, but all the nissen join together to ring the bells on Christmas Eve. This is also the time to set out the *juleneg*, a sheaf of corn hung in the trees for the birds to eat.

The Danish Christmas tree is decorated with handmade wooden ornaments, glazed-paper hearts, angels, and Danish flag garlands. Santa Claus or the father of the house distributes gifts, and the family joins hands to sing and dance around the tree.

The wrapping of Christmas gifts possibly originated in Denmark. The Danes like to disguise the gifts by wrapping them in ways that prevent children from guessing what is inside. They include many layers of paper. Each layer contains a different name so the gifts keep changing hands. Often there is no gift inside, but rather a note giving some clue as to where the real gift is hidden. The time of gift opening is exciting and lengthy.

Epiphany marks the end of the holiday in Denmark. The tree is taken down. Young unmarried women are supposed to walk backwards to bed to ensure good dreams of the men they will marry.

ACTIVITIES

1. Read "The Last Dream of the Old Oak Tree," a Christmas tale by Hans Christian Andersen (Danish). Also read *Kirsten's Surprise: A Christmas Story* by Janet B. Shaw.
2. Read and show the picture book *The Tomten* by Astrid Lindgren. The fine illustrations and story help children visualize the Scandinavian climate and the secretive nature of the tomten.
3. Let the students write their own tomten or nisse stories. Think about all the mischief they might cause! Have them illustrate their stories and display them in the school library.
4. Go Julebukking! Let students dress up in costumes to completely disguise themselves and pantomime hints about who they are. Go to another classroom and let those students try to guess. Enjoy a Scandinavian treat together.
5. Make St. Lucia and Star Boy figures. Directions and patterns can be found on pages 70-71.
6. Dress as St. Lucia or Star Boy. Costume directions can be found on page 72.
7. Make a Scandinavian straw ornament. See page 73 for directions.
8. Have fun with a mischievous nisse. Directions for making one can be found on page 74.
9. Scandinavian Christmas Breads abound! Some are thin and pliable while others are thin and crisp. Still others resemble fruited breads or coffee cakes. Regardless of the form, Scandinavians enjoy these energy-rich foods which help them stay warm in the winter time. A Swedish recipe for lussekattes can be found on page 75. Check cookbooks for other bread recipes.
10. Scandinavian Christmas carols and a prayer can be found on page 76.
11. Make a garland of national flags. Choose a country, locate the image of its flag, and then have each student make one flag (about the size of an index card). String them together on yarn. Hang the garland around the classroom or on a Christmas tree.

St. Lucia and Star Boy Figures

Materials:

- 2 one-piece clothespins (or craft store doll pins)
- white felt
- green felt
- 6" (15 cm) red ribbon or rickrack
- 6" (15 cm) blue ribbon or rickrack
- 2½" (6.25 cm) green pipe cleaner
- two 4" (10 cm) white pipe cleaner
- five 1" (2.5 cm) squares white paper
- yellow marker
- fine-line markers for facial features
- many 4" (10 cm) pieces yellow embroidery floss
- white craft glue
- white embroidery floss, yarn, or other hanger
- blue construction paper
- gold foil star stickers
- patterns (page 71)

Directions for St. Lucia:

1. Glue yellow floss strands to the center top of a clothespin for hair.
2. Bend the green pipe cleaner into a circle, slightly twisting or overlapping the ends. Glue this "wreath" on top of the hair.
3. Twist and glue a white pipe cleaner around the "body" just below the shoulders to form two arms. Bend the arms so they stick out from the sides.
4. Use the pattern to cut a gown from white felt.
5. Spread a bead of glue around the neck of the doll and attach the gown. Overlap the edges at the back.
6. Cut small holes for the arms and pull them through. Trim the arms if necessary.
7. Tie a red belt at the doll's waist, gathering extra fabric into soft even folds around the body.
8. Roll the white papers into tiny "candles." Add a drop of glue to hold each closed. Use yellow marker to color the top ⅛" (.3 cm) to look like a flame.
9. Slightly bend the bottom of each candle. Glue each at regular intervals to the wreath on St. Lucia's head.
10. If desired, draw facial features with fine-line markers.
11. To make an ornament, add a hanger of white floss or yarn to the backside of the figure.

Directions for Star Boy:

1. Follow steps 3–6 above.
2. Tie a belt of blue trim as in step 7 above.
3. Cut the hat pattern from blue construction paper. Attach star stickers to decorate. Tape or glue the hat into a cone shape and glue onto Star Boy's head.
4. Follow steps 10–11 to complete.

St. Lucia and Star Boy Figures *(cont.)*

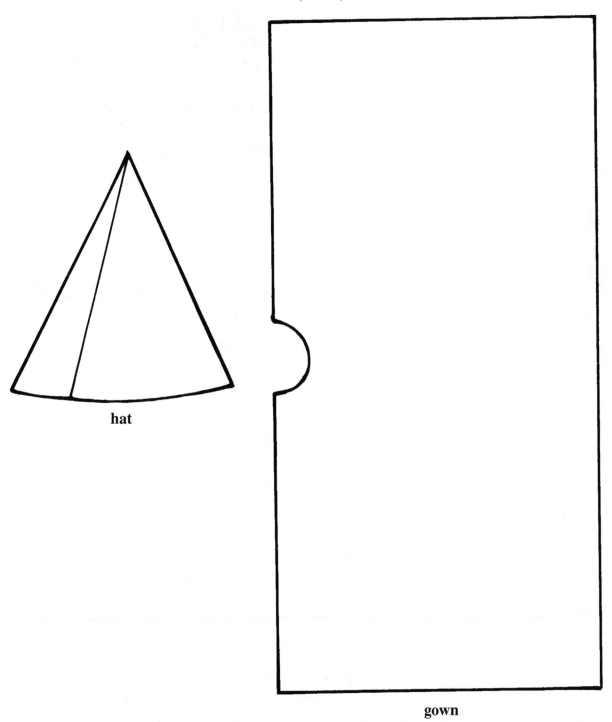

hat

gown

ST. LUCIA AND STAR BOY COSTUMES

Children may dress up as St. Lucia and Star Boy, too. On December 13, these students can serve a platter of goodies! Use large white t-shirts or dress shirts with belts for the costumes. To make a child-sized headdress, follow these directions.

Materials:

- green poster board
- 18" x 24" (45 cm x 60 cm) blue construction paper
- yellow, white, green, and red construction paper
- yellow tissue paper
- scissors
- tape
- leaf pattern (page 129)
- star patterns (page 129)
- elastic cording (optional)

Directions for St. Lucia's Wreath:

1. Using the green poster board, cut an oval shape about 12" (30 cm) long and 10" (25 cm) wide.
2. Cut out the center to fit the top of a child's head (like a hat brim), leaving approximately a 3" (7.5 cm) border around.
3. Clip the inner oval at 1" (2.5 cm) intervals and fold these upward. Try it on—it should fit snugly around the forehead.
4. Make 5–7 candles by rolling white paper into 5" x 3" (12.5 cm x 7.5 cm) tubes. Overlap the ends of each tube and tape together.
5. Make several 1" (2.5 cm) clips at the base of each candle and bend outward.
6. Tape the candle bases to the oval and push small wads of yellow tissue paper into the top ends of the candles.
7. Cut leaves from green construction paper. Cut small circles from red paper to make berries. Glue these to the top of the wreath covering the candle bases.

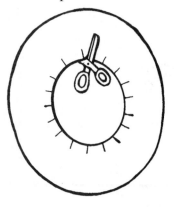 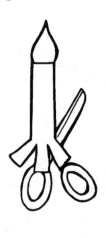 

Directions for Star Boy's Hat:

1. Make a cone-shaped hat from blue construction paper. Start with the full sheet and twist into a cone shape until the opening fits the top of the child's head. Tape the edges together and trim off the excess. Trim the opening so it is even.

2. Trace and cut stars from yellow construction paper and glue them to the hat.

3. Add some elastic cording if needed for a chin strap.

SCANDINAVIAN STRAW ORNAMENT
Materials:
- straw from rye, wheat, or oats (obtain from a local farmer or purchase at a craft store)*
- red crochet thread, yarn, or ribbon
- white or tan thread
- warm water in a tub
- hairspray
- scissors
- ruler
- needle
- glue
- dish soap (optional)

Directions:
1. Cut off the heads of the grain, leaving at least a 1" (2.5 cm) stem and straw lengths of 10–12" (25–30 cm). (Do not throw away the heads.)
2. Soak the straw in warm water for two hours or until pliable. **Optional:** Add a few drops of dish soap to soften the straw shafts.
3. Tie three (or six) pieces of straw together at one end.
4. Braid the entire length of the straw, using single or double strands.
5. Form the braid into a wreath, overlap the ends, and wrap the ends together securely with thread.
6. Put the remaining grain heads into two bunches and insert them crisscross at the base of the wreath. Use some glue if needed.
7. Spray with a thin coat of hairspray.
8. Tie a red ribbon into a bow to cover the ends and add some color.
9. Add loop of thread to the back for a hanger.
10. **Variation:** Do not cut off grain heads. Use pieces which are about 14" (35 cm) long. Tie three pieces together 1" (2.5 cm) from the cut end. After braiding to within 1" (2.5 cm) of the head ends, loop together into a tear drop shape and tie the ends together where the braiding ends. Apply a red bow at the tie. Hang with the grain heads down.

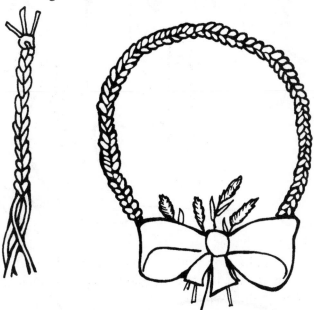

*Note: If you cannot find appropriate grains to use, purchase a package of raffia at a craft store. This goes a long way, can easily be cut to desired lengths, and is very easy to braid.

NISSE

Materials:

- patterns (below)
- white poster board or other heavy paper
- markers or crayons
- pencil
- scissors
- glue

Directions:

1. Duplicate or trace the nisse pattern onto the poster board. Cut out.
2. Color. (Nisse usually wear dull red hats and mittens, brown pants, and green shirts. Their beards are white.)
3. On the blank sign held by the nisse, print the name of the individual to whom he belongs.
4. Cut out the stand, fold it on the dotted lines, and glue it to the back of the nisse.
5. To perch the nisse on a bowl, omit the stand and cut him along the heavy lines of the shoes. Bend him slightly to sit on the bowl's rim. To display the nisse in a window, omit the stand and tape him in a window corner. To hang the nisse as an ornament, omit the stand and poke a hole in the top of the nisse's hat, adding a thread loop.
6. **Follow-up Activity:** Play "Hide the Nisse." The teacher hides one or more nissen while the students are out of the room. When they return, the students try to find the nissen. Each finder gets to do something special.

Lussekattes

These delicious buns are served in Sweden on December 13, the Feast of St. Lucia. The oldest daughter, dressed as St. Lucia, carries the buns to her family. This recipe makes one dozen buns.

Ingredients:

- 1 package dry yeast
- $\frac{1}{4}$ c. (65 mL) very warm water
- additional water (to brush on buns)
- $\frac{1}{2}$ c. (125 mL) milk, scalded, then cooled
- $\frac{1}{4}$ c. (65 mL) sugar
- additional sugar (to sprinkle on buns)
- $\frac{1}{4}$ c. (65 mL) margarine (softened)
- additional margarine (softened to spread on buns)
- 2 eggs
- $\frac{1}{2}$ t. (2.5 mL) ground cardamom
- pinch saffron (or yellow food coloring)
- $\frac{1}{2}$ t. (2.5 mL) salt
- $\frac{1}{2}$ t. (2.5 mL) grated orange peel
- 3 to $3\frac{1}{2}$ c. (750 to 875 mL) flour
- additional flour
- raisins

Lussekattes *(cont.)*

Preparation:

1. Dissolve yeast in warm water.
2. Stir in milk, sugar, margarine, 1 egg, cardamom, saffron, salt, and orange peel.
3. Stir in $1\frac{1}{2}$ c. (375 mL) flour and beat until smooth.
4. Stir in enough remaining flour to make dough easy to handle.
5. Turn out onto a floured surface and knead 5–10 minutes.
6. Place in greased bowl, turn, and cover. Let rise in a warm place until double in size (about $1\frac{1}{2}$–2 hours).
7. Punch down the dough. Divide into two portions and cut each portion into six pieces.
8. Shape each piece into a smooth rope about 10-12" (25-30 cm) long.
9. Shape each rope into an "S" shape and curve both ends into a tight coil. Place one raisin in the center of each coil. (See the illustration.)
10. Place on greased cookie sheets. Brush the tops with margarine.
11. Let rise in a warm place for 30–45 minutes.
12. Heat the oven to 350° F (180° C). Brush the buns with an egg/water mixture and sprinkle the tops with sugar.
13. Bake for 15–20 minutes or until golden brown. Serve warm.

THY LITTLE ONES

Thy little ones, dear Lord, are we
And come Thy holy bed to see.
Enlighten every soul and mind
That we the way to Thee may find.

JEG ER SAA GLAD HVER JULEKVELD *(Norwegian)*

Jeg er saa glad hver Julekveld,
Thi da blev Jesus fodt;
Da lyste Stjernen som en Sol
Og Engle sang saa sodt.

I AM SO GLAD FOR CHRISTMAS EVE *(English)*

I am so glad for Christmas Eve,
The day of Jesus' birth.
My heart is full of joy untold
In Yuletide story old.

A TABLE PRAYER *(Norwegian)*

I Jesu navn gar vi til bords
At spise og drikke pa dit ord.
Dig Gud til aere, oss til gavn,
Sa far vi mat i Jesu navn.
Amen.

A TABLE PRAYER *(English)*

In Jesus' name, we go to the table
To eat and drink at your word.
Your God to honor, us to be gifted,
So we get food in Jesus' name.
Amen.

Spain

Felices Pascuas! Merry Christmas from Spain!

Some Christmas festivities in Spain begin in early December, such as bringing evergreens indoors and opening the many outdoor Christmas markets. However, Christmas Eve is the beginning of the real holiday. It extends through the full twelve days of Christmas to January 6.

Since Spain is predominately Catholic, Christmas is quite religious. Life-sized Nativity scenes decorate public places. Midnight mass and *Los Pastores* (mystery plays which show the shepherds' adoration of the Christ Child) are important Christmas Eve events. Lights and *luminarias* (see pages 49–50) abound, and of course, there is feasting and gift-giving as the Three Kings deliver presents to children on the night of January 5.

Outdoor markets open in early December, selling *zambombas* (drums), tambourines, small guitars, and other musical instruments that will accompany groups of people as they sing the *villancicos,* old sacred songs sung at the mystery plays and throughout the holiday. Families also enjoy creating their own *nacimiento* or *belen* (manger scene), indicating the true start of the season.

Christmas Eve is called *la Noche Buena* (the Good Night). When December 24 arrives, the people fast all day, and they will not eat until after midnight. Bells chime loudly to call people to midnight mass. The church service may include a "Mass of the Rooster" as a reminder of the old legend about the rooster's Christmas message. It says that on the night of the Christ Child's birth, a rooster flew to the top of the stable and proclaimed the birth to the world by crowing, *"Cristo nacio!"* ("Christ is born!"). The miracle continued when another rooster added, *"En Belen!"* ("In Bethlehem!")

When church services are over, the people feast on *paella* (a rice and seafood dish), an abundance of fresh fruits, *turron* (a hard candy), *chirimoyas* (custard apples), and a king's cake. They may even celebrate with fireworks!

The remainder of Christmas Day is often spent with family and friends. Cakes and other desserts are exchanged. Young children recite Christmas verses and sing songs as they go from door to door, hoping for small toys or sweet treats. But Epiphany is the time for real gift-giving. Children write letters to the Three Kings and set their shoes under their beds or on their balconies. They may leave hay for the tired camels. In the morning, they awaken to find toys and fruit overflowing their shoes!

The grand finale comes on Epiphany. There is the special parade of kings and animals up and down the streets. Then, with music and merriment, the holiday season ends.

ACTIVITIES

1. Read "The Three Magi" found in *An American Christmas* (Allied Books Ltd.) Using a world map, trace the path of the Three Kings on their journey from the Orient to the land of Spain. Let the children illustrate this story.
2. Have a parade around the room or around the school. Play musical instruments and sing Christmas songs. See pages 78–79 for instrument directions and page 80 for song lyrics.
3. Write letters to the Three Wise Kings telling of Christmas wishes. Share them with the class.

ACTIVITIES *(cont.)*

4. Make paella, Spain's most popular dish. It usually contains a variety of seafood with saffron, rice, and chicken. Find a Spanish cookbook and vary the ingredients to suit your budget and tastes. A simple and inexpensive version might include only chicken. To add seafood, try some canned varieties such as clams and small shrimp.

5. Make custards. These come in a wide variety of flavors and preparation methods, many of which are too difficult in a classroom. If you have some willing volunteers, it might be fun to sample some custards which have been prepared at home.

6. Make turron. A recipe follows on page 79.

7. Make splatter paintings to represent Spain's Christmas fireworks.

TAMBOURINE

Materials:

- plastic ice cream lid or aluminum pie plate
- bells or metal soda pop rings
- hole punch
- yarn

Directions:

1. Punch holes around the edge of the lid or pie plate, about 1" (2.5 cm) apart.

2. Cut a piece of yarn to 24" (60 cm).

3. Weave yarn in and out of the holes in the lid or pie plate, and each time the yarn is on the outer edge, thread on one or two bells or pop top rings. (Variation: Use two lids or pie plates and weave them together, enclosing dried beans or popcorn inside for added sound.)

4. When you reach the starting point, tie the yarn securely into a knot. If desired, cut several more pieces of yarn to add as streamers.

5. Shake to make music.

SHAKER

Materials:

- unpopped popcorn, dried beans, jingle bells, or soda pop tops
- any disposable plastic container and lid
- masking tape

Directions:

1. Put about ¼ c. (65 mL) popcorn, beans, etc. into the container.

2. Attach the lid firmly and seal with masking tape.

3. Shake to make music.

ZAMBOMBA

Materials:

- cardboard oatmeal box or plastic food container with lid
- pipe cleaner or yarn
- hole punch

Directions:

1. Punch two holes near the top of the container, 2" (5 cm) apart.
2. Put a pipe cleaner or yarn through the holes and twist or tie into a loop for the handle.
3. Attach the lid securely.
4. Decorate if desired.
5. Hold the drum by the handle with one hand and tap on it with your fingertips to make music.

Turron

This hard candy is a favorite in Spain at Christmastime.

Ingredients:

- 2 c. (500 mL) blanched almonds, toasted
- ¼ c. (65 mL) honey
- 7–8 oz. (200-250 g) block of ready-made marzipan
- ½ c. (125 mL) sugar
- powdered sugar

Preparation:

1. Grease a 6" x 9" (15 cm x 22.5 cm) pan.
2. Break up the marzipan with your fingers.
3. Turn the broken marzipan onto a clean surface dusted with powdered sugar. Knead for 5 minutes or until smooth.
4. Set this aside.
5. Combine the almonds, sugar, and honey in a saucepan and cook over a low heat until the sugar dissolves. Stir constantly.
6. Increase the heat and bring the mixture to a boil. Cook for 3 minutes, stirring constantly.
7. Remove from the heat and stir in the prepared marzipan. Beat until well mixed.
8. Spoon the mixture into the baking pan and cool for 5 minutes.
9. With a knife, score candy into 1½" (4 cm) squares. Cool completely.
10. When cooled, remove the candies from the pan and break them into squares along the score lines. Eat or wrap in waxed paper to store until needed.

VILLANCICO (SPANISH)

Vamos todos a Belen
Con amor y gozo.
Adoremos al Senor,
Nuestro Redentor.

VILLANCICO (ENGLISH)

Let us all go to Bethlehem
With love and joy.
Let us adore the Lord,
Our Redeemer.

OLD SPANISH CAROL

Shall I tell you who will come
To Bethlehem on Christmas Morn,
Who will kneel them gently down
Before the Lord, newborn?

One small fish from the river
With scales of red, red gold,
One wild bee from the heather,
One gray lamb from the fold,
One ox from the high pasture,
One black bull from the herd,
One goatling from the far hills
One white, white bird.
And many children—God gave them grace,
Bringing tall candles to light Mary's face.

Shall I tell you who will come
To Bethlehem on Christmas Morn,
Who will kneel them gently down
Before the Lord, newborn?

Switzerland

There are four nationalities and languages spoken in Switzerland: German, French, Italian, and Romansh (Swiss). Because of this, the greetings and customs vary throughout the small country.

In some parts of Switzerland, the Christmas celebration begins on December 5 with a parade called the "Pursuit of St. Nicholas." Marchers carry huge cardboard headdresses above their heads. These resemble lace-patterned bishops' hats, and they are worn in honor of St. Nicholas. With bells ringing and brass bands playing, the marchers escort St. Nicholas into town. On December 6, St. Nicholas rides through town and gives a speech. This is followed by a festive meal for the whole town.

In many parts of Switzerland, children receive their gifts on Christmas Eve from *Wienectchind* or *Christkindl* (the Christmas Child). Wienectchind wears a white robe and carries a lantern through town. Six girls in pink dresses accompany him to visit families, sing, and share cookies and cakes with the children.

In French areas, gifts are given on New Year's Day. In still other areas, Father Christmas gives gifts to boys, and his wife Lucy provides gifts to girls.

Bells are important in Switzerland's celebrations. All kinds of bells can be heard, including cowbells, sleigh bells, and church bells. The Christmas tree is decorated with gold and silver garlands, blown-glass ornaments, wrapped cookies, and fruits and nuts. A star is perched on top.

ACTIVITIES:

1. An old tradition to predict weather is still practiced in some parts of rural Switzerland today. Try this yourself. The mother or grandmother of the household finds the biggest and best onion. She cuts it in two. She peels off twelve layers to represent the twelve months of the year, and she lines them up in order. She fills each layer with salt and lets it stand all night. In the morning, she checks each piece. Those peels that have dry salt indicate fair weather for that month. Those peels that contain wet salt indicate rainy weather. What do your results show? Keep a weather chart for the rest of the school year and compare actual results to your predictions.

2. Learn to say "Christmas" in the four languages of Switzerland:

   Weihnachten (German)

   Noël (French)

   Natale (Italian)

   Nadel (Romansh/Swiss)

3. Make and hang a special Christmas garland. String letters spelling "Christmas" in as many languages as you can find. Letter patterns can be found on pages 97–99.

4. Make a Christmas bell. Directions can be found on page 82.

5. Make a bishop's headdress ornament. Directions can be found on pages 82–83.

CHRISTMAS BELL

Materials:

- 2 clean tin cans of different sizes (smooth any rough edges)
- hammer
- roofing nail
- 12" (30 cm) pipe cleaner (metallic silver is best)
- jingle bells (optional)

Directions:

1. Pound the nail into two spots on the tops of the tin cans to create two holes in each.
2. Bend the pipe cleaner in half and push the two ends through the holes in the smallest can, working from the inside to the outside. (Optional: Before threading the pipe cleaner, string one or two jingle bells and move to the center of the cleaner. Twist several times.)
3. Pull the pipe cleaner ends out until they are even and twist twice at the top of the can.
4. Straighten the pipe cleaner ends and line them up with the holes in the larger can. Insert the smaller can into the larger can as you push the pipe cleaner ends through the holes in the latter.
5. Pull the pipe cleaner ends out. Let the smaller can hang out below the lower edge of the larger can about 1–2" (2.5–5 cm).
6. With one hand, hold the protruding pipe cleaner ends, and twist the smaller can four times with the other hand.
7. Twist the protruding pipe cleaner ends together four times near the top of the can.
8. To make a hanger, overlap and twist the ends of the pipe cleaners together.

BISHOP'S HEADDRESS

Materials:

- red or white construction paper
- markers or crayons
- glue
- thread
- paper doilies
- cotton balls
- tape
- patterns (page 83)

Directions:

1. Trace the headdress pattern twice onto construction paper.
2. Place a section of doily to cover the entire outline of each headdress half. Use the doily as a stencil. Hold it down in one place on each headdress half as you color over the area.
3. Lift the doily to see the pattern left. Repeat if desired.
4. Trace the cylinder pattern onto construction paper. Cut it out, roll it, and tape it as shown.
5. Run a bead of glue along the sides and top of the headdress halves and press them together. Let dry five minutes.
6. Carefully place a few cotton balls inside the hat to give it a 3-D effect.
7. Place the cylinder halfway into the hat and glue it in place as shown (next page).
8. Poke a small hole in the top of the hat and tie a loop of thread to hang.

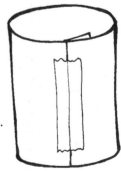

Bishop's Headdress

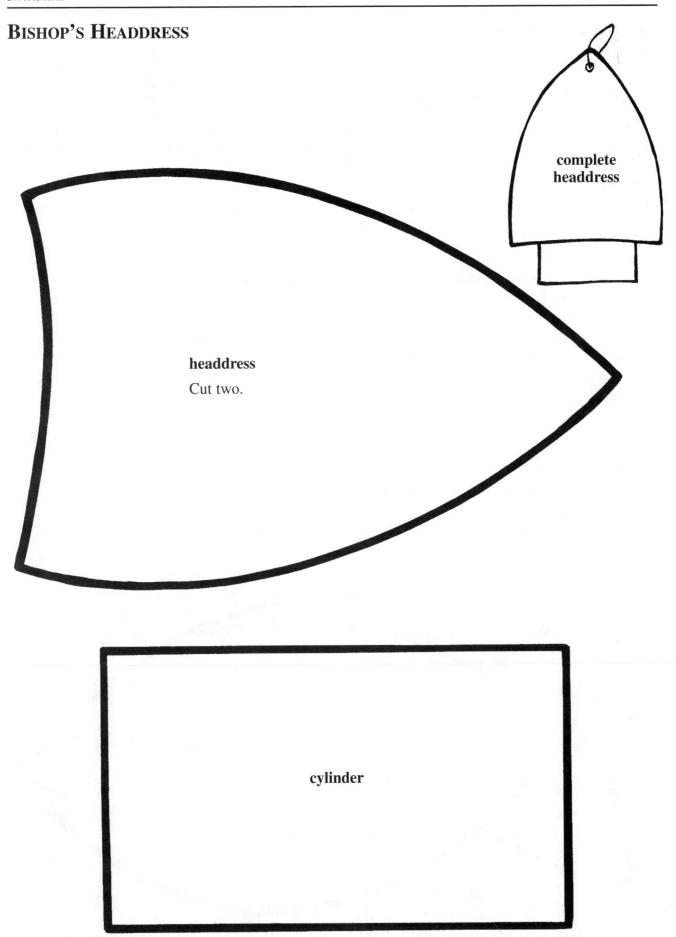

complete headdress

headdress

Cut two.

cylinder

Thailand

Most people in Thailand are Buddhist, so Christmas is not a major holiday. However, those who do celebrate it enjoy caroling on Christmas Eve. Hot drinks, candies, and cakes are given to the singers. Most other Christmas activities take place within the church. It is decorated with a tree, garlands of crepe paper, and a full-size manger scene. Ornaments are often made of woven straw. Because of its importance to Thailand, the Christian symbol of the fish is an obvious ornament choice.

ACTIVITY

Make a fish ornament. Follow the directions below.

FISH ORNAMENT

Materials:

- burlap or other rough woven fabric
- typing paper
- wide markers
- glue
- fish pattern
- scissors
- 2 cotton balls
- yarn

Directions:

1. Place the pattern on top of the burlap. Rub a light-colored marker with pressure over the entire pattern until the texture of the burlap shows clearly. Repeat with a sheet of typing paper.

2. Remove the burlap. With a dark-colored marker, emphasize the outline and details of the fish.

3. Put the pattern sheet on top of the colored typing paper, wrong sides together. Cut the fish shape through the typing paper so the two match exactly.

4. Run a bead of glue around the edges of the wrong side of one fish piece. Set the cotton in the middle of the fish, and then place the other fish piece on top of the cotton and glue, lining up all edges evenly. Press. Let dry.

5. Add a loop of yarn and hang as a decoration. (If you can, add the bottom of the yarn loop before gluing the two sides together.)

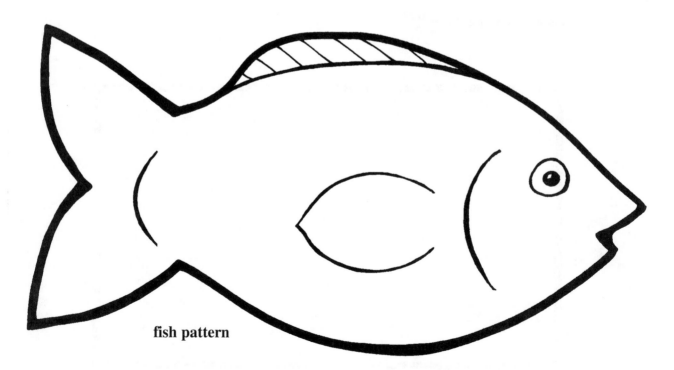

fish pattern

Ukraine

This formerly communist country has many characteristics in common with Czechoslovakia and Russia, yet it has some unique customs as well. Of most interest is the Ukrainian Christmas tree which wears a spider web for good luck. There is a legend about a poor woman who had nothing to put on her children's Christmas tree. She felt sad that her children could not enjoy the holiday. But in the morning, the tree branches were covered with spider webs. When the sun rose, they turned to silver. She was no longer poor in material things or in spirit.

ACTIVITY:

1. Make a spider web ornament. Directions for two versions can be found below and on page 86.

SPIDER WEB ORNAMENT *(Easy)*

Materials:

- 6" (15 cm) square black poster board
- web pattern (or own drawing)
- scissors
- white chalk
- white glue
- silver glitter
- pencil
- yarn

Directions:

1. Use a pencil to transfer the web pattern onto the square of black poster board. This can be done by coloring the back of the pattern with white chalk and then tracing the pattern while it is placed chalk-side-down on the black paper.
2. Run a thin bead of glue along all pencil lines.
3. Sprinkle glitter over all glue until well-coated. Let dry one to two hours.
4. Use scissors to trim around the outside line of the web, leaving a ¹/₂" (1.25 cm) border.
5. Make a small hole at the top and thread a 6" (15 cm) piece of yarn. Tie to make the hanger.

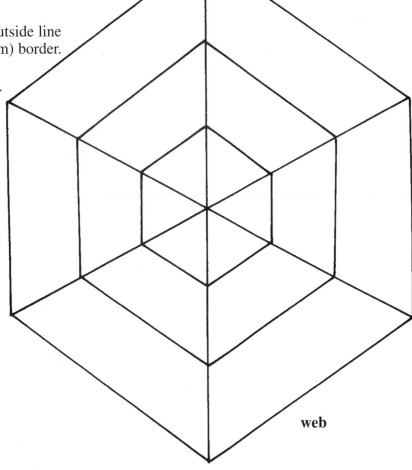

web

Spider Web Ornament *(Difficult)*

Materials:

- metallic silver and white crochet yarn
- 6" (15 cm) square black poster board
- blunt needle with large head
- web pattern
- white chalk
- scissors
- pencil

Directions:

1. Trace the web pattern onto the black poster board as directed in the previous activity.
2. With the needle, poke a small hole at every dot on the pattern.
3. Thread the needle with a 24" (60 cm) piece of crochet yarn and tie a knot in one end.
4. "Sew" the web by bringing the needle up through hole 1, down through the center hole, up through hole 3, down through center hole, up through hole 5, down through center, and so forth. You should have a six-pointed star.
5. Next, sew the outer edges. Up at 1, down at 3; up at 5, down at 7; up at 9, down at 11. Now reverse the pattern: up at 11; down at 9, up at 7; down at 5, up at 3, down at 1. Your outer edge is complete.
6. Sew the inside lines in the same manner until all lines are covered with thread. Try to catch the "star" threads with those going around the web for a better shape. Add new thread as necessary. Tie a knot on the back when complete.
7. With scissors, trim off the excess black paper, leaving a ½" (1.25 cm) border.
8. Hang with a loop of crochet yarn attached to one outside hole.

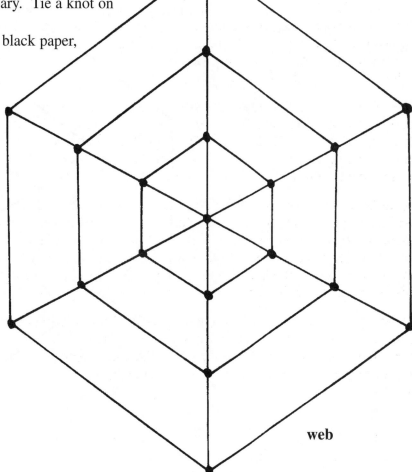

web

United States and Canada

As Canadians and Americans busily prepare for Christmas, feelings of joy, charity, and "hustle and bustle" abound. Although most of the celebrations occur during the week between Christmas and New Year's Day, the preparations begin much earlier. Shopping often begins in early November, followed by baking in December. Advent wreaths and calendars mark the beginning of Christian celebrations in churches and homes. Santa Claus, Christmas trees, cards, presents, carols, feasting, and lights are all important parts of a North American Christmas.

Christmas customs in both the United States and Canada are a combination of those from the other countries in this book. Immigrants to the countries brought their favorite traditions. In the United States, many of these have been adopted and personalized to make them "American." In Canada, the tendency is for cultural groups within the nation to maintain their own traditions.

"Ho, Ho, Ho! Merry Christmas!" This is the sound of Santa Claus and his helpers preparing for Christmas. Santa originated with the Dutch St. Nicholas, *Sinter Klaas.* Santa delivers gifts to the good boys and girls on Christmas Eve as they dream of happy surprises. He and Mrs. Claus live at the North Pole with lots of little elf helpers. All year long, they design and make special gifts which are loaded onto a sleigh on Christmas Eve. Pulled by his eight famous reindeer, Santa flies through the air and lands on each rooftop. He slides down the chimney (or enters via some other mysterious way) and leaves small gifts in the stockings the children have hung by the fireplace. Larger gifts are set under the Christmas tree. These images of Santa became part of cultural folklore when Dr. Clement C. Moore wrote a poem for his children called "A Visit from St. Nicholas." Thomas Nast drew illustrations of this jolly man as he made toys, filled stockings, and drove his reindeer-pulled sleigh. Nast's pictures became very popular and now represent the usual depiction of Santa Claus.

Santa visits with children throughout the holiday season. He can be seen in shopping malls and department stores where children take turns sitting on his lap and sharing their lists of wishes. He also appears in many television shows and movies. Children write letters to Santa stating their requests, telling of their good behavior, and perhaps wishing him a Merry Christmas.

The Christmas tree, originally from Germany, is found everywhere in the United States and Canada today. Temporary Christmas tree lots display hundreds of precut evergreens, and many families put theirs up as early as the day after Thanksgiving. There are also Christmas tree farms where families go to select and cut their own tree. Live potted and artificial trees are becoming more popular as an environmental alternative to cutting down trees.

Regardless of the type of tree chosen, the trees are always decorated and placed in a prominent spot in the home. Ornaments often reflect the family's ethnic heritage as well as recent history. Many are handmade by children and friends. Most well-known are the cranberry and popcorn garlands strung by little hands and placed lovingly around the tree. Some trees are elaborately decorated to fit a theme, and in many places there are special festivals to display these unique creations. In addition, holly, ivy, mistletoe, and the poinsettia are all popular Christmas plants.

Christmas cards originated in England but have become a major custom in the United States and Canada. There are thousands of commercially-produced varieties: religious and secular, serious and humorous, traditional and contemporary. Sending greetings to friends and family has become a popular way to stay in touch with those who live far away.

UNITED STATES AND CANADA *(cont.)*

The giving of gifts has become big business. Stores often make their most significant profits for the whole year in the month between Thanksgiving and Christmas. No longer are small gifts of fruits, nuts, cookies, and simple toys the norm. Each year, the gifts seem to become more elaborate and expensive until the space beneath the tree is overflowing with wrapped packages. But handmade gifts from local Christmas bazaars are also popular. (These have German roots.)

Of course, whether simple or elaborate, the true spirit of giving has not been lost. There is much charity during the holiday season, from putting money in the red iron pots of the Salvation Army bell-ringers to giving money, clothing, and baskets of food to those who are less fortunate.

Christmas carols from around the world are enjoyed by Canadians and Americans. They are played on radio stations throughout the month of December, and many people have several Christmas records, cassettes, and compact discs in their homes. It has become popular in recent years for some high-profile recording artists to donate their time and talents to the production of recorded Christmas music, with the profits from sales going to charitable organizations.

As in most other nations, the Christmas season is a time for good food and fellowship. Many dishes in Canada and America are direct contributions from other countries, though some, of course, have national origins. For example, the American Indians introduced cranberry relish and roast turkey to the early settlers, and they have remained a traditional part of the Christmas meal. Frosted sugar cookies, candy canes, and fudge are typical holiday desserts today. Eggnog and hot cider are enjoyed by many throughout the holidays. Canada, which has a strong French base, often enjoys many French foods at this time of year.

Light is a symbol of Christmas throughout the world, and Canadians and Americans have elaborated on the simple candle. Strings of colorful lights are displayed outdoors on public buildings, homes, and trees as well as indoors on Christmas trees and windows. The popularity of Mexican and Spanish *luminarias* is spreading as well.

Celebrations in Canada and the United States are largely the same; however, there are a few distinctions. Most particularly, Boxing Day (page 32) is of great importance to Canadians, whereas most Americans do not celebrate it or its customs. Canada also houses a large Dutch population. The Dutch there tell of *Sleipner,* and eight-legged horse that delivers Christmas gifts. The Canadians of Ukrainian descent also have their own tradition. In the course of their Christmas meal, they throw a combination of wheat and honey to the ceiling. If it sticks, they say they will have good luck in the coming year. Finally, the Inuit children of Canada hope to see Santa arrive in a sleigh pulled by cows and horses. Reindeer for them are commonplace, whereas cows and horses are not.

Many Christians celebrate the season of Advent, lighting a candle on the Advent wreath on each of the four Sundays before the holiday and a fifth candle on the holiday itself. Prayers are said and songs are sung. Christians often celebrate Christmas itself with an evening church service on Christmas Eve and a morning service on Christmas Day. Then families and friends join together in feasting and celebrating. The rest of the week between Christmas and New Year's Day may be filled with ordinary activities as well as parties. On New Year's Eve and Day the celebrations are sometimes repeated, this time usually for non-religious reasons, though some denominations celebrate the New Year as well. Epiphany, too, though not a commercial holiday, is still celebrated by a number of Christian religious groups. With the New Year and Epiphany usually comes the close of the holiday season.

ACTIVITIES

1. Read "A Visit from St. Nicholas" by Dr. Clement C. Moore. It can be found in most anthologies of Christmas stories. Also read "The Gift of the Magi" by O. Henry. This is a nice way to introduce the practice of gift-giving.

2. With older students read the chapter called "A Merry Christmas" from Louisa May Alcott's *Little Women*. Younger students will enjoy the chapters dealing with Christmas in Laura Ingalls Wilder's *Little House in the Big Woods, Little House on the Prairie,* and *Farmer Boy.* Compare and contrast the March, Ingalls, or Wilder family's Christmas with a Christmas celebration today.

3. Let the students write about their upcoming Christmas plans. Describe family traditions or favorite holiday activities. These can be glued to the back of Christmas pictures the students draw or paint. Roll the pictures and tie them with ribbons as gifts for parents.

4. Brainstorm for things that describe Christmas. Have children write similes or explain the following: as slow as Christmas, lit up like a Christmas tree, as cold as Christmas.

5. Make a classroom Santa's workshop. Elf hats can be made from construction paper cones. Let students choose craft items to make for family members. Set up work stations with materials and instructions, as well as a gift-wrapping area with wrapping paper, gift tags, and so forth. Allow the students plenty of time to make and wrap gifts to give.

6. Play the "Candy Cane Toss" game. To play, create two simple green cardboard wreaths with inside openings of at least 8" (20 cm). Make two "candy canes" by twisting red and white pipe cleaners together. Divide into two teams. Hang the wreaths from the ceiling at the students' eye level. Each team will line up behind a wreath, and each player will toss the team's candy cane into the team's wreath, run up to retrieve it, and then hand it to next player on the team. The first team to finish gets to hand out small candy cane treats to the other team and themselves.

7. Create a Christmas scene as a group project. Attach mural paper to a wall area to make approximately a 6' (2 m) square work space. After brainstorming about various American or Canadian Christmas settings and the details in each one, let groups of children re-create each with markers, glue, construction paper, fabrics, felt, and other available materials. It is best to make a rough sketch before beginning. Display. Some possible settings to make include the following: a fireplace and stockings, Santa's workshop, winter, sledding, caroling, Santa and his sleigh in flight, a decorated Christmas tree with gifts beneath, and holiday shopping or gift-giving.

8. Make Christmas cards. Directions can be found on page 90.

9. Make Christmas stocking to hang in the classroom. See page 90 for directions and page 91 for a pattern. You might add a festive touch by creating a giant fireplace out of construction paper and cardboard. Hang the stockings around it, or make miniature versions to hang on the tree.

10. As a class, decorate a small tree with your own Christmas garland. See page 92 for some simple garland directions.

11. A simple gift idea is a festive light bulb pin. Directions can be found on page 92.

12. Recipes for cranberry relish, popcorn balls, and sugar cookies are on pages 93 and 94.

13. Several famous Christmas songs originated in America. "Go Tell It on the Mountain" is a spiritual that originated with the slaves in the South. An American wrote "We Three Kings" more than one hundred years ago. Several secular songs are also American. Among these are "Jingle Bells," "Rudolph the Red-Nosed Reindeer" (a commercial hit for Gene Autry), "I'm Dreaming of a White Christmas," and "Jolly Old Saint Nicholas." Enjoy singing these songs as a class. The words to the first two can be found on page 95.

CHRISTMAS CARDS

Materials:

- construction paper
- patterns (pages 126–136)
- scissors
- glue
- markers, paints, crayons, etc.

Directions:

1. After discussing Christmas celebrations in the U.S. and Canada, design and send a special card to someone who might be lonely during the holidays. Consider nursing homes or veterans' hospitals.
2. Make the cards from the above materials or any others you would like.
3. Hand deliver the cards, if possible, and sing some carols.

CHRISTMAS STOCKING

Materials:

- red or green construction paper or felt
- hole puncher
- shredded newspaper
- stocking pattern (page 91 or 134)
- red, white, or green yarn
- scissors
- cotton balls
- large-eyed needle (if using felt)

Directions:

1. Cut out the stocking pattern.
2. Trace and cut out two stockings from red or green paper or felt.
3. If using paper, punch holes around the outside about $1/2$" (1.25 cm) apart.
4. Lace together with a contrasting yarn. If using felt, sew with a needle.
5. If desired, glue cotton balls to the top area of the stocking, the toe, and the heel.
6. If making an ornament, add a yarn loop to the top and hang your stocking.

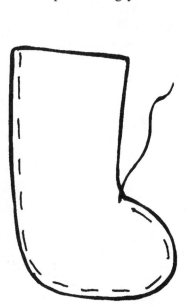

CHRISTMAS STOCKING *(cont.)*

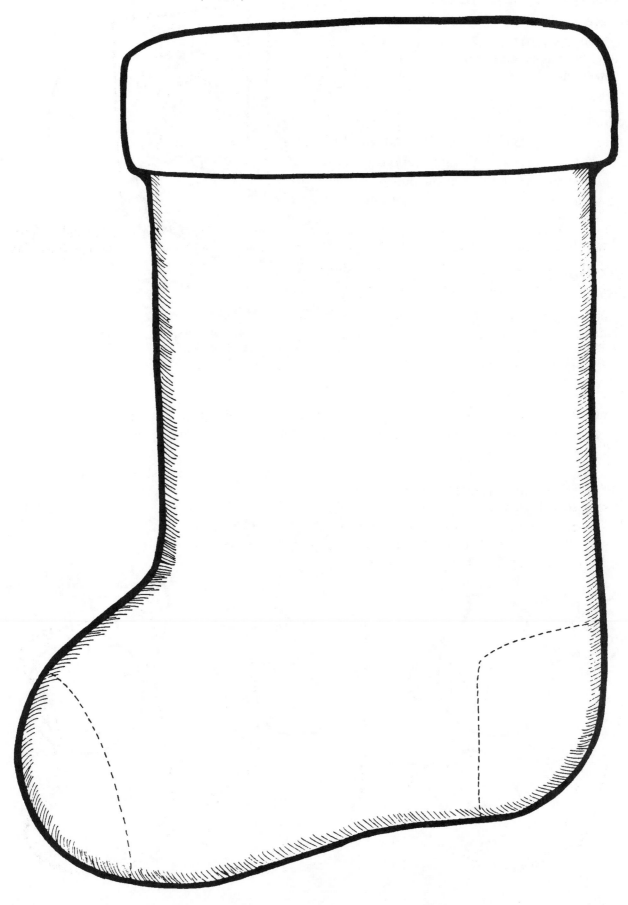

POPCORN AND CRANBERRY GARLAND

Materials:
- whole cranberries
- day-old popped corn
- sewing needle
- thread

Directions:
1. Thread the needle with at least 24" (60 cm) thread.
2. String on berries and popcorn in various patterns.
3. Tie off at the end and start a new thread.
4. Tie all lengths together when finished and clip off any excess thread.
5. Decorate a tree or room.

LIGHT BULB PIN

Materials:
- small colored light bulb (burned out)
- narrow red or green ribbon
- safety or jewelry pin
- thick craft glue
- tiny artificial ivy leaves (optional)

Directions:
1. Tie a ribbon bow on the metal portion of the bulb. Add glue if necessary.
2. Glue a piece of ivy onto the bow.
3. Glue the pin to the back of the bulb and it let dry. To make an ornament instead of a pin, do not add the pin, but instead attach a thread hanger.
4. Wear or hang and enjoy!

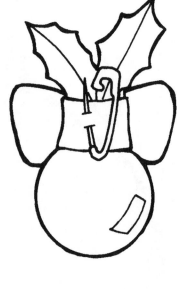

Cranberry Relish

This Christmas dinner treat is part of the legacy of Native Americans. It makes a delicious side dish with roast turkey.

Ingredients:
- 1 pound ($^1\!/_2$ kg) whole cranberries
- 2 c. (500 mL) sugar
- 2 oranges (washed and quartered)
- 2 apples (washed and quartered)
- 1 T. (15 mL) lemon juice

Preparation:
1. Grind the cranberries in a food grinder. Students can take turns turning the handle of an old-fashioned grinder.
2. Grind the oranges and apples in the food grinder.
3. Stir all the ground fruits together with the sugar and lemon juice.
4. Cover and refrigerate overnight.

Popcorn Balls

Popcorn balls are a traditional American Christmas favorite.

Ingredients:
- 4 quarts (4 L) unsalted popped popcorn
- 1 c. (250 mL) sugar
- 1 c. (250 mL) white syrup
- 1 package red or green gelatin
- powdered sugar

Preparation:
1. Combine sugar, syrup, and gelatin in a saucepan and bring to a boil. Boil and stir constantly for two minutes.
2. Pour the above combination over the popped corn and stir quickly.
3. With wet hands, press the popcorn into balls. (The mixture is hot, so use caution.)
4. If too sticky to eat, roll in powdered sugar.
5. Wrap in clear plastic and tie with ribbon for decorations and gifts.

Rolled Sugar Cookies

These traditional Christmas cookies can be made the old-fashioned way or the easy way by using pre-made cookie dough from the grocery store. This recipe makes 4–5 dozen cookies.

Ingredients:

- 1¼ c. (315 mL) sugar
- ½ c. (125 mL) shortening
- 2 t. (10 mL) vanilla extract
- ½ t. (2.5 mL) salt
- 3 T. (45 mL) sour cream (optional)
- ½ c. (125 mL) butter or margarine
- 2 eggs
- 3 c. (750 mL) flour (plus extra for rolling)
- 2 t. (10 mL) baking powder

Preparation:

1. Lightly flour a clean pastry cloth and rolling pin cover. Preheat oven to 375° F (190° C).
2. Cream sugar, butter, and shortening until fluffy.
3. Beat in vanilla. Add sour cream if desired.
4. Add flour, salt, and baking powder. Mix well.
5. Roll about ⅓ of the dough at a time to about ⅛–¼" (.3–.6 cm) thickness. Cut with any desired cookie cutters.
6. If you wish to hang the cookies on the Christmas tree, before baking poke a hole with a small straw or toothpick in the top of each.
7. Bake for seven to ten minutes or until lightly golden on the bottoms.
8. Remove from the cookie sheet. Frost when cool.

Frosting for Sugar Cookies

You may wish to make this frosting from scratch, or you can use purchased icing as well as other candies and decorative toppings.

Ingredients:

- 3 T. (45 mL) white shortening (softened) or butter (if color does not matter)
- 1 t. (5 mL) clear vanilla or almond extract
- 1–2 T. (15–30 mL) milk
- powdered sugar (enough to make the right consistency for spreading)
- food coloring

Preparation:

1. Combine margarine, vanilla, and milk in a bowl. Add powdered sugar, ½ c. at a time, and beat until spreadable.
2. Divide into small bowls and add food coloring as desired.
3. Frost the sugar cookies. Let the frosting set.
4. Store the cookies for eating or string with thread to hang.

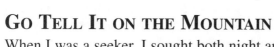

GO TELL IT ON THE MOUNTAIN

When I was a seeker, I sought both night and day,
I sought the Lord to help me, and He showed me the way.

Refrain: Oh, go tell it on the mountain, over the hills and ev'ry where.
Go tell it on the mountain that Jesus Christ is born!

He made me a watchman upon the city wall
And if I am a Christian, I am the least of all.

Refrain

WE THREE KINGS

We three kings of Orient are
Bearing gifts we traverse afar,
Field and fountain, moor and mountain,
Following yonder star.

Refrain: O, star of wonder, star of night,
Star with royal beauty bright,
Westward leading, still proceeding,
Guide us to thy Perfect Light.

(Melchior) Born a King on Bethlehem's plain,
Gold I bring to crown Him again,
King forever, ceasing never,
Over us all to reign.

Refrain

(Caspar) Frankincense to offer have I,
Incense owns a Deity nigh,
Pray'r and praising, all men raising,
Worship Him, God most high.

Refrain

(Balthazar) Myrrh is mine,
   its bitter perfume,
Breathes a life of gathering gloom,
Sorrowing, sighing, bleeding, dying,
Seal'd in the stone-cold tomb.

Refrain

Glorious now behold Him arise,
King and God and Sacrifice,
Alleluia, alleluia,
Earth to the heav'ns replies.

Refrain

General Activities

This section of the book includes cross-curricular activity ideas, puzzles, and patterns which are either generic or incorporate more than one country's customs. They are outlined below.

1. **ABC's of Christmas:** As a class, brainstorm a list of alphabetical Christmas words. For example, *A* is for *angels, B* is for *bells,* and so forth. You might also make this a game by having individual students or student teams complete the alphabet on their own and then compare answers. Award one point for each appropriate word or for a word no one else has.

2. **Name That Carol:** In teams, try to name familiar carols after hearing just two or three notes, or play part of a carol and let a team sing or say the next phrase of the song. Award points if desired, and award bonus points if the team can name the country of origin!

3. **Musical Chairs:** Play this traditional game using Christmas carols.

4. **Merry Christmas Word Scramble:** Write the words *Merry Christmas* on the board. Challenge students to find other words using only these letters. You might do the same with a Christmas greeting in another language. Make this a classroom competition if you like.

5. **Shape Stories:** Let students draw and describe something relating to Christmas in the shape of the thing described. For example, in a gift shape a student might draw and write about the gift wanted most for Christmas, or in a tree shape a student can draw and describe a beautiful Christmas tree.

6. **Christmas in _____:** Let the students choose a country they enjoyed studying. They can write about the holiday celebrations in the country chosen and then decorate (color) a tree accordingly. Use the tree pattern on page 126.

7. **Advent Calendar:** Students can surprise each other with handmade Advent calendars. To make one, instruct the students to do the following.

   Draw a Christmas scene on a large piece of paper. Then, draw 24 three-sided boxes on the picture. Make each box the same size: 1" (2.5 cm) across the top and bottom and ³/₄" (2 cm) along the right side. Number the boxes in any order you like from 1–24. Color the picture, making sure you can still see the lines of the boxes. Now, cut the boxes so that they become little doors opening from right to left. This is tricky, so be very careful. (Remember, do not cut down the left-hand side!) Next, draw 24 little Christmas pictures the same size as the little doors. Cut out each little picture leaving a thin border around it. This is so that the paper each picture is on is actually larger than each door. Tape or glue each little picture behind a door of the big picture so that when the door is opened, the picture can be seen. Exchange with a friend, and on each of the 24 days before Christmas, open one door in sequence.

   Variation: Instead of little pictures, write Christmas greetings or put tiny photographs of family and friends behind each door.

8. **Christmas Greetings:** Make Christmas garlands by stringing the letters of Christmas greetings from around the world. Use pre-made bulletin board letters or have students make and color their own. (Patterns can be found at the bottom of page 97 as well as on pages 98 and 99.) Each of the following phrases say "Merry Christmas."

   Glaedelig Jul (Norway/Denmark)   *Feliz Natal* (Brazil)
   Happy Christmas (England)   *Buon Natale* (Italy)
   Hauskas Joulua (Finland)   *Joyeux Noël* (France)
   Felices Pascuas (Spain)   *Meri Kurisumasu* (Japan)
   Wesolych Swiat (Poland)   *Feliz Navidad* (Mexico)

GENERAL ACTIVITIES (cont.)

9. **Wordsearches:** Pages 100–101 have two delightful wordsearches for students to enjoy.

10. **Dear Santa:** Use page 102 to write personal letters to the Christmas gift bearer of your choice.

11. **Christmas Bingo:** Play the traditional game with a Christmas twist. Use pages 103–104.

12. **Christmas Codes**: Decode the secret Christmas code on page 105. Students can also make up some of their own.

13. **Christmas Math:** Entertaining math worksheets for various skill levels are on pages 106–108.

14. **Christmas Science:** On page 109 find a variety of science activities.

15. **Christmas Geography:** Page 110–113 offer a number of ways to practice geography skills with a Christmas theme.

16. **"Christmas Around the World" Student Booklets:** Page 114 can be reproduced several times for each primary student. On each page, the student can write an interesting bit of Christmas information about a specific country and draw a picture pertaining to that country and information. Together the pages can make a booklet for each student. Older students will need copies of pages 115–125. They can color these booklets, study them, and add information to them. You might choose to reproduce the pages with only the country name and let the students complete the information as they study each country. To make the booklet, reproduce those pages desired, then have the students fold them on the dotted lines with the printed sides of each page together. (For example, the information about Germany will face the corresponding Christmas tree illustration.) There is one exception: the cover page folds in the opposite way from the rest of the pages. Once folded, staple the pages together along the fold.

17. **Christmas Patterns:** The patterns on pages 97–99 and 126-136 can be used for the activities throughout this book as well as for decoration, art work, clip art, book covers, unit awards, stationery, and so forth. Reproduce as necessary. You might also enlarge the patterns. If your copy machine does not have the ability to do this, use an overhead projector to project the image onto a piece of paper attached to the wall. Move the projector in order to get the size you want, and then trace the image. (Note: Whenever possible, encourage students to draw their own figures.)

18. **Wrapping Paper:** Students can design and paint their own wrapping paper. Use the patterns from pages 126–136 to cut Christmas shapes from sponges. Dip the sponges in tempera paints of medium consistency, and then stamp the sponges on sheets of butcher paper. Let dry. Add glitter, if desired.

"CHRISTMAS GREETINGS" LETTERS

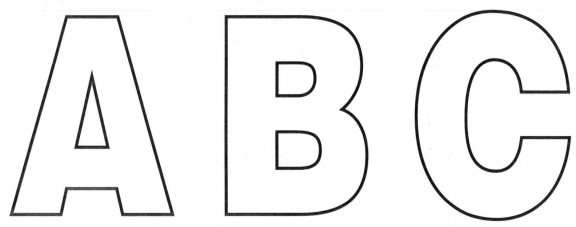

"CHRISTMAS GREETINGS" LETTERS *(cont.)*

"CHRISTMAS GREETINGS" LETTERS *(cont.)*

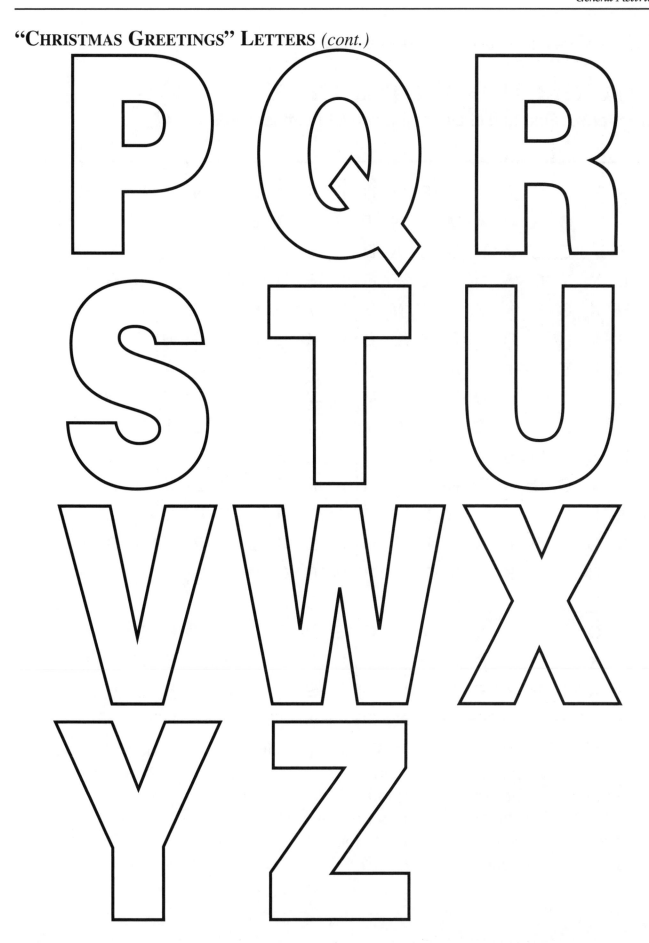

Name_____

Christmas Wordsearch

Directions: Find and circle the hidden Christmas words.

```
S  K  J  D  S  F  H  E  J  H  F  K  D  S  G  N  D  K  S  R  K
A  T  O  R  N  A  M  E  N  T  B  C  R  E  E  D  N  I  E  R  D
E  F  O  G  Z  H  Y  S  A  D  A  S  O  P  S  A  L  J  K  X  S
L  Y  T  C  A  N  D  L  E  G  K  F  D  V  P  A  S  O  G  V  A
H  K  G  P  K  Z  P  E  M  E  P  I  P  H  A  N  Y  L  O  D  I
S  M  N  O  R  I  S  S  C  B  D  K  L  J  P  G  W  E  O  G  N
A  L  V  G  L  E  N  A  D  V  E  N  T  O  O  E  A  Y  D  N  T
L  G  I  I  C  D  R  G  L  M  M  V  Q  W  E  L  U  N  W  E  L
O  B  E  T  T  D  K  G  O  Y  A  S  E  L  K  L  I  T  I  O  U
H  E  H  M  S  A  R  H  R  I  F  L  D  R  E  F  K  U  L  T  C
C  L  C  B  A  E  R  R  A  N  A  F  E  B  G  Z  X  B  L  E  I
I  L  E  H  E  D  H  N  C  T  I  O  D  R  T  R  D  K  L  L  A
N  O  R  T  F  A  S  D  G  H  N  D  R  E  H  P  E  H  S  T  K
T  B  C  A  K  T  V  R  E  B  M  E  C  E  D  M  L  E  Z  S  B
N  K  D  E  A  B  G  L  A  S  H  G  S  U  E  S  S  I  N  I  L
I  Q  F  R  A  N  K  I  N  C  E  N  S  E  O  P  H  G  F  M  B
A  K  D  W  H  D  O  R  N  S  H  L  F  I  R  L  D  B  E  U  W
S  A  I  F  K  R  A  I  T  T  E  S  N  I  O  P  H  S  B  K  D
```

Advent	carol	frankincense	nisse	Saint Nicholas
angel	creche	gold	ornament	shepherd
Befana	December	good will	poinsettia	star
bell	Epiphany	Las Posadas	present	stocking
candle	evergreen	mistletoe	reindeer	wreath
cards	feast	myrrh	Saint Lucia	Yule

100

Name

Who Are the Gift Bearers?

Directions: Find and circle the names of the Christmas gift bearers from the countries around the world.

```
H S I G S S A M T S I R H C N A M D L O H J K
K L F T Y R O G N F L I S A B T N I A S X O T
R K C H R I S T M A S C H I L D G D N A Z D H
I S I N T E R K L A A S G S I U R U M M C N R
S S T K J U L T O M T E N C D C H N I T D I E
S U V A B D K G L T S N B N R J U C A S G H E
K A S D R M K L U U F J I S G T R H K I V C K
R L N G R M E B B U K K W E D S R E M R C T I
I C A D I O A A S S T I D R N L G L C H C C N
N A O H N S M N E S S I N L U J C A V C M E G
G T A A M B T E I P E T R A W Z B O M R V N S
L N P C I P E R E N O E L E R N E R M E C E V
E A F N O H H O T E I O S H O N F E A H M I D
P S O B B C M B A B O U S C H K A N Z T C W K
C S V A T Y M I K A L A S O P G N X Z A T J F
K B D G L S A L O H C I N T N I A S C F O R T
```

Babouschka	Père Noël
Befana	Saint Basil
Christkind	Saint Nicholas
Christmas Child	Santa Claus
Dun Che Lao Ren	Sinter Klaas
Father Christmas	Star Man
Gesú Bambino	Svaty Mikalas
Hoteiosho	Three Kings
Julnisse	Wienectchind
Jultomten	Zwarte Piet
Kriss Kringle	
Old Man Christmas	
Papa Noël	

Dear Santa

Directions for the Teacher: Have each student write and send a letter to Santa or any of the other Christmas gift bearers they have learned about. Duplicate the form below the dotted line.

Dear _____,

Love,

102

Christmas Bingo

Directions for the Teacher: Duplicate a bingo card and a set of symbols (page 104) for each student. Let the students cut and paste (or draw freehand) the Christmas symbols in each box. They will not use all the symbols.

To play, call out the symbol names one at a time. (Draw them from a hat or bag.) Students can place red hot candies or other markers on each symbol when it is called. Play as usual, deciding ahead of time whether you are playing for a line, black out, or four corners.

Variation: Have the students write math problems, spelling words, or numbers in the boxes, and then play bingo as before.

Christmas Bingo

Christmas Bingo *(cont.)*

 angel

 Befana

 bell

 candle

 candy cane

 Christ Child

 church

 donkey

 dove

 elf

 gingerbread

 gift

 holly

 Joseph

 lamb

 light bulb

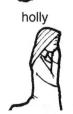 Mary

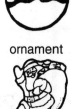 ornament

 poinsettia

 reindeer

 rose

 Santa Claus

 shepherd

 sleigh

 snowflake

 snowman

 stable

 stocking

 Three Kings

 tree

 wooden shoe

 wreath

Name _____

Christmas Codes

Directions: Using the symbol code for the alphabet, figure out the secret message. Then, write some of your own!

_____ _____ _____ _____ _____ _____ _____ _____ _____ _____

_____ _____ _____ _____ _____ _____ _____ _____

_____ _____ _____ _____ _____ _____

Name _____

Dot-to-Dot Two-by-Two

Directions: Count by two's to follow this dot-to-dot.

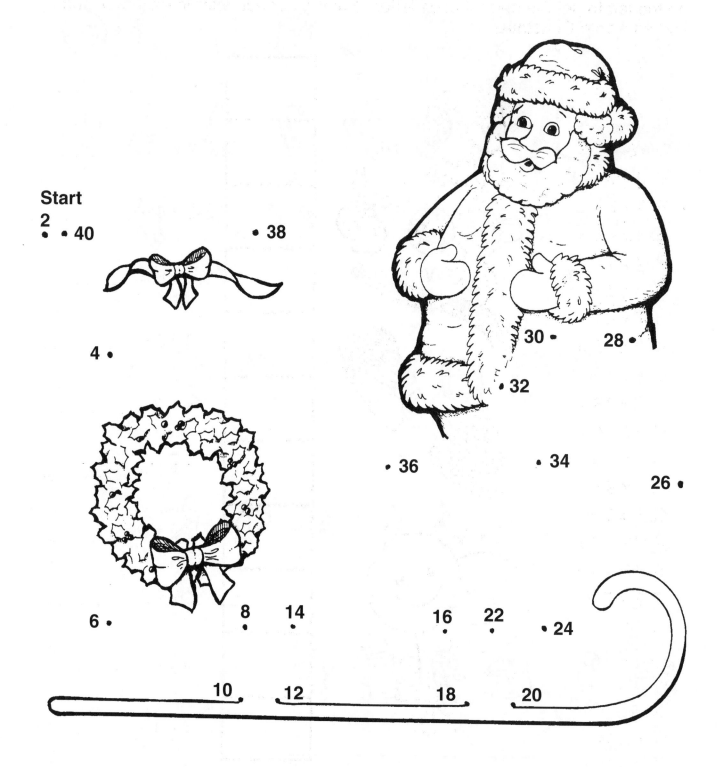

Start
2
• • 40   • 38

4 •
                                                    30 • •   28 •

                                                          • 32

                              • 36   • 34
                                                                        26 •

6 •   8   14   16   22   • 24

          10   12   18   20

Name _____

Math Code Munchies

Directions: Solve the problems on the left to find the code number for each letter. Then, solve the problems on the right. Match the answers to the answers on the left to get the correct code letter. Put the correct letter in each box and find a favorite Christmas treat.

A. $27 \div 9 =$

B. $30 \div 5 =$

C. $27 \div 3 =$

D. $48 \div 4 =$

E. $2 \times 9 =$

F. $3 \times 7 =$

G. $48 \div 2 =$

H. $4 \times 7 =$

I. $6 \times 5 =$

J. $4 \times 8 =$

K. $2 \times 17 =$

L. $6 \times 6 =$

M. $2 \times 19 =$

N. $10 \times 4 =$

O. $45 \div 3 =$

P. $3 \times 9 =$

Q. $5 \times 7 =$

R. $12 \div 6 =$

S. $16 \div 4 =$

T. $2 \times 7 =$

U. $64 \div 4 =$

V. $5 \times 4 =$

W. $6 \times 7 =$

X. $5 \times 9 =$

Y. $4 \times 12 =$

Z. $7 \times 7 =$

$6 \times 4 =$ _____

$2 \times 15 =$ _____

$5 \times 8 =$ _____

$3 \times 8 =$ _____

$3 \times 6 =$ _____

$4 \div 2 =$ _____

$2 \times 3 =$ _____

$2 \times 1 =$ _____

$36 \div 2 =$ _____

$9 \div 3 =$ _____

$3 \times 4 =$ _____

Name _____

Gift-Wrapped Math

Directions: Start with the first problem on the left. Following the ribbon, use the answer from the first problem as the beginning of the problem in the next box. Continue to follow the ribbon from box to box, using the answers as you go. Put your final answer in Santa's chimney.

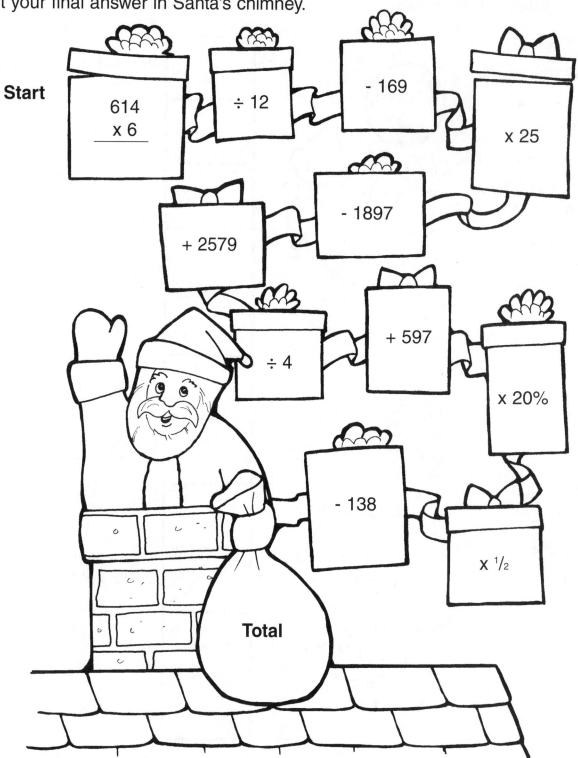

Start

614
x 6

÷ 12

- 169

x 25

+ 2579

- 1897

÷ 4

+ 597

x 20%

- 138

x ½

Total

Science Discoveries and Explorations

1. **Christmas Greenery:** Collect and study samples of evergreen branches (Douglas fir, white spruce, black spruce, blue spruce, Virginia pine, and balsam), pine cones, holly, ivy, and mistletoe. Accomplish this by soliciting them from the children's families and Christmas tree farms or nurseries. Once you have an array of holiday greenery, do the following.

   Set up an interesting table display. Include pictures, maps, and reference books that give information about each type of greenery. (Check the bibliography in this book for titles related to Christmas trees.) Label each sample with the correct name and the area in which it is grown. Let the children examine all with magnifying glasses. Encourage students to compare the appearances of the needles, branches, pine cones, berries, and leaves. They should use their senses to touch and smell each one.

   After a day or two of exploration, check the students' understanding by removing your labels. Students should try to label and identify each sample and then check for accuracy. Short oral or written reports can be assigned so that each student can teach the rest of the class about an assigned or favorite type of evergreen or greenery.

2. **Christmas Blooms:** There are other plants grown especially to bloom at Christmastime. Find some of the following: amaryllis, ardisia, azalea, begonia, Christmas cactus, Christmas pepper, cyclamen, gloxinia, kalanchoe, poinsettia, and streptocarpus.

3. **Holiday Feeder:** Give a Christmas gift to the birds and animals surrounding your school and home. (This is a tradition in many European countries.) As a class, make and hang a bird feeder outdoors and watch the birds who frequent it. You will need yarn, fat needles, cranberries, raisins, popped popcorn, and stale bread. Now, do the following.

   a. Cut a piece of yarn about 24" (60 cm) long.
   b. Thread the yarn onto a needle and knot one end.
   c. String a variety of cranberries, raisins, popcorn, and chunks of stale bread.
   d. When you reach the end of the yarn, remove the needle and knot the end.
   e. Drape the garland of bird food on the branches of a nearby tree.

   You can make simple animal feeders in a similar fashion. To feed these creatures, make a garland feeder similar to the steps above, except use chunks of carrots, apples, or other fruits and vegetables. Drape it on the low branches of a nearby evergreen tree.

4. **Follow-up Chart:** Check the feeders described above and record the findings each day. Chart the foods that disappear first, the quantities consumed each day, the tracks found (if visible), and the types of animals and birds identified at the feeders most often and/or least often.

   Before actually making the charts, you might consider having the students make predictions ahead of time. They will have fun seeing how accurate their predictions prove to be.

Name _____

Where Are We?

Directions: Read each problem below. Use an atlas, almanac, or other reference materials to answer the questions.

1. If Santa plans to visit the smallest U.S. state first and work his way up to the largest, which state would he visit first? Which would he visit last? Use a U.S. map and trace the route you would pick for Santa to follow.

   Challenge: Use resource materials to compare state sizes. List all 50 and Washington, D.C., in increasing order of size, either by population or area.

2. If Santa flies from Norway to Newfoundland, which ocean must he cross?

3. The children in Los Angeles, California, are just getting up to see if Santa has been there. It is 7:00 A.M. Do you think the children in Philadelphia, Pennsylvania, are up? Why or why not?

4. Choose one country in this book and find a picture of its flag. Using construction paper or crayons, reproduce it and make a display in your classroom. Then do some research about the symbols in each flag. Why did each country choose these colors and shapes?

5. Why do you think so many Christmas traditions in Canada and the United States come from European countries?

6. Assuming Santa visits every good girl and boy, and assuming all the children have been very good, in which city of the world will Santa and his helpers have to spend the most time?

   Math Challenge: Compare that city to five other cities of the world. Figure out what percentage of time needs to be spent in each. (For example, if City A has a population of 10 million and City B has a population of 3 million, 30% of the time spent in City A will be spent in City B.)

110

Did You Know?

Directions for the Teacher: Share these interesting tidbits and activities with your students.

- Christmas celebrators in Liberia, Africa, cut down oil palms and decorate them with red bells. Find a picture of this palm tree and visualize what Christmas might be like in Liberia. Make a decorated palm from green and red construction paper and display it in your classroom.

- Many children who live in South America find their gifts in a cradle or crib to remind them of the manger in which Jesus slept. Others may leave hay in their shoes for the camels since they believe the Three Kings deliver their gifts. Make a baby's cradle or a manger. Use heavy paper, glue, markers, and so forth to construct your own design.

- There is a special food eaten in Puerto Rico that resembles a gift. At Christmas, Puerto Ricans wrap the leaves of a tropical fruit, called a plantain, around a pork filling, and they tie it with string. The "packages" are boiled and served. Find a picture of a plantain.

- In Ghana, Africa, Father Christmas comes from the jungle instead of the North Pole.

- In Columbia, South America, children play a game to get gifts. Each child tries to say "Aguinaldo" first, because the loser must give the winner a small treat. *Aguinaldo* means *Christmas gift.* Try this game yourselves!

- In Syria, the Christian children believe an animal brings their Christmas gifts. It is the camel belonging to Jesus, which happened to be the youngest camel traveling with the Wise Men.

- The Christmas cactus comes from Brazil. It has beautiful red blossoms that bloom just in time for Christmas each year. Find a picture of this plant or bring one to school to watch it bloom.

- When Santa visits Korea, he carries gifts in a wicker basket on his back. Korea's Christmas is much like Christmas in the United States and Canada. There are decorated trees, Christmas displays in stores, gift exchanges, and Christmas Eve services complete with caroling and festive meals. Eat rice cakes and *kimchi* in honor of a Korean Christmas.

- In Australia, the people often have a picnic for Christmas Day supper. It is summertime during the Christmas holiday there, which means it is very hot and dry. And Santa rides on water skis! Have an (indoor) picnic for lunch to remind you of Australia's Christmas.

- *Carol* means *circle dance.* In many countries, the people traditionally dance around the Christmas tree while singing their favorite carols. Try it!

- The tallest cut Christmas tree recorded was 221' (66.3 m) tall and was displayed in a mall in Seattle, Washington. When playing outside, pace off 221' (66.3 m) to see how tall that tree was.

- Nicholas, the saint who gave inspiration for today's Santa Claus, was born in Turkey. Use reference books to find out about the country of Turkey.

- In areas of India where there are no evergreen trees, the Christians make their own trees from whatever materials they have. It may be a bundle of rice straw covered with clay and standing 6' (1.8 m) tall! With lighted candles stuck into the clay and colorful paper chains surrounding it, it is truly beautiful.

- In the Middle Ages, children's gifts came in bundles of three: one was rewarding, one was useful, and one was for discipline. What gifts would you suggest?

Name _____

Searching for Christmas

Directions: Use any available resources (including a zip code directory) to respond to the following questions and prompts.

1. Which states in the United States contain each of these towns? (The number of towns with each name is given in parentheses.)

   Christmas (1) _____

   Mistletoe (1) _____

   Rudolph (1)_____

   Santa Claus (1) _____

   Snowflake (1) _____

   Noel (1)_____

   North Pole (2) _____

   Star (4) _____

   Star City (2) _____

   Antler (1)_____

   Holiday (1) _____

   Carol City (1) _____

2. Find the zip code for each town listed above.

3. Using state maps, locate each town.

4. If you would like a letter (or letters) to be postmarked from one of these towns, first address it and affix a stamp. Then, place the letter in a larger envelope (a group of letters may go together) and send it to "Postmaster" with your request. He or she will postmark the letter and send it to the address you have already written on it!

5. Use an atlas, state maps, or almanac to find other city names which remind you of Christmas or another theme. Compile a list.

Note to the Teacher: See page 140.

Ethnic Settlements in the United States

Directions for the Teacher: Use this list of cities and towns to gather more information about the cultures they embody. Write letters to each Chamber of Commerce or the person listed in your almanac. Ask about Christmas customs and traditions, special foods, typical ethnic names, and other things in which the students are interested. Solicit pictures, recipes, and travel guides. Locate these cities on a map and brainstorm why these groups settled where they did. Compare the weather and topography of these cities with those of the native lands.

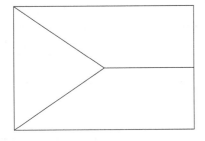
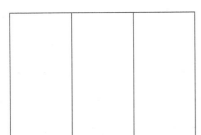

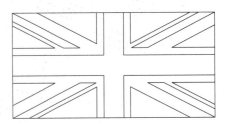

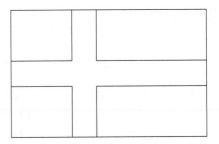
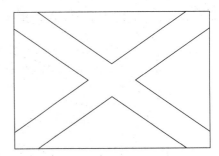

Czechoslovakian Settlements
 Cedar Rapids, Iowa
 Protivin, Iowa

English Settlements
 Fairmont, Minnesota
 LeMars, Iowa
 Runnymede, Kansas

Dutch Settlements
 Pella, Iowa
 Orange City, Iowa
 Holland, Michigan

French Settlement
 Ste. Genevieve, Missouri
 New Orleans, Louisiana

German Settlements
 Milwaukee, Wisconsin
 LaCrosse, Wisconsin
 Frankenmuth, Michigan

Italian Settlement
 New York, New York

Mexican Settlements
 Los Angeles, California
 Sante Fe, New Mexico
 Albuquerque, New Mexico

Norwegian Settlements
 Spring Grove, Minnesota
 Little Norway, Wisconsin
 Decorah, Iowa

Scottish Settlement
 Traer, Iowa

Swedish Settlement
 Lindsborg, Kansas

Spanish Settlements
 Montevidio, Minnesota
 Austin, Texas

Swiss Settlement
 New Glaris, Wisconsin

Christmas Around the World

_____
(country)

_____
- -
_____
_____
- -
_____
_____
- -
_____

See page 97 for directions.

Christmas Around the World

This book belongs to

_____.

GERMANY

Froliche Weihnachten! That is how to say *Merry Christmas* in German. The people of Germany love Christmas, and they have many traditions. The Christmas tree comes from Germany as well as the carol "O Christmas Tree." When you see a gingerbread house or eat a gingerbread cookie, think of Germany for that is where gingerbread originated.

On Christmas Eve, families decorate their trees, go to church, eat good food, and open gifts. *Kriss Kringle* or *Weihnachtsmann* (the Christmas Man) delivers gifts to the good children. *Hans Trapp* brings switches to those who have been naughty!

GREAT BRITAIN

The English greeting is *Happy Christmas!* England has given the world many Christmas carols and some famous Christmas stories. Charles Dickens' *A Christmas Carol* and the song "The Twelve Days of Christmas" are English. Christmas cards were first sent in England and today are an important part of Christmas in many places throughout the world. It is Father Christmas who brings gifts to children in England. He may carry a bowl of wassail and visit homes during the twelve days of Christmas between Christmas and Epiphany. December 26, Boxing Day, is also an important day in England. On this day, gift boxes are given in gratitude to community workers.

FRANCE

In France, the greeting is *Joyeux Noël!* There are many wonderful foods eaten during the French holidays. Gift-giving may have originated in France in the name of St. Nicholas. On December 5, French children leave their shoes by the fireplace and hope that Père Noël will secretly leave presents. The *crèche* is the name of the French manger scene. The handmade figures inside are called *santons*. The crèche is the most important holiday decoration for the French family. Puppet shows are popular with children, and eating wonderful desserts and crusty breads is popular with everyone.

SPAIN

People in Spain say *Felices Pascuas!*, and Christmas is *Navidad.* Christmas Eve and Day are full of religious traditions. Nativity scenes, church services, and mystery plays called *Los Pastores* are important events. Music is everywhere, and families set up their own manger scenes called *nacimientos* or *belens.* *Luminarias* light the way for the Holy Family.

The Spanish celebration extends through January 6, Epiphany. This is when children receive their gifts. Children set out their shoes on the evening of January 5. They are filled with hay for the camels, and the Three Kings replace the hay with gifts they secretly deliver. There is a big parade on January 6, and this ends their holiday.

ITALY

Merry Christmas in Italian is *Buon Natale!* The first true Christmas carols probably came from Italy, and the first manger scene was set up in this country by St. Francis of Assisi. It is called a *presepio.* Some such scenes are very large and fancy. The manger always remains empty until Christmas Eve when the Christ Child is gently placed inside.

Most children do not receive their gifts until January 6. La Befana brings them. She rides a broomstick from house to house searching for the Christ Child and leaving gifts for all good children. Some children also receive gifts on Christmas Eve from *Gesú Bambino* (Baby Jesus), although in some homes Santa may deliver them. The Italians enjoy good foods and family gatherings throughout the Christmas season.

NETHERLANDS

The people of the Netherlands are famous for bringing *Sinter Klaas* to the world. His name is the origin of the name *Santa Claus.* In the Netherlands, Sinter Klaas arrives on a white horse and brings *Zwarte Piet* (Black Peter) along as his helper. Black Peter writes down the names of naughty children in his big red book. He also carries the bag full of treats to be given to good children. Dutch children set out their wooden shoes on December 5 and leave carrots or hay for Sinter Klaas' horse. In the morning, they find their surprises. Family gifts are also surprises, wrapped in many layers of paper. Fast poets called *sneldichters* write funny, personalized poems to go with the gifts.

SCANDINAVIA

These four Scandinavian countries have cold weather at Christmastime, and their traditions reflect this. Beautiful Christmas trees, good foods, clean homes, and gifts are all important. Each country has a little elf or gnome who delivers gifts to children on Christmas Eve. In Sweden, it is *Juletomten.* In Norway and Denmark it is *Julenisse.* Both are tiny and mischievous.

The Feast of St. Lucia is held in Sweden. The oldest daughter in the family wears a white robe and a wreath of greens and candles on her head as she serves special breakfast buns to her family. Star Boys escort her. Trees in Scandinavia are decorated with garlands of flags. Bowls of *gröt* (porridge) are set out for the elves, and fish, gröt, and a variety of desserts are enjoyed by everyone.

AUSTRIA

The people in Austria celebrate for the entire month between St. Nicholas Day and January 6, Epiphany. "Silent Night," the most popular Christmas carol in the world, originated in Austria, and marzipan is enjoyed as a tasty dessert here and across Europe.

Christkind is the gift giver, and he leaves presents unwrapped under the tree to be received on Christmas Eve. Sometimes people hang their trees upside down in a special corners! It is usually decorated with paper ornaments, nuts, apples, and candles.

SWITZERLAND

There are four languages spoken in Switzerland—German, French, Italian, and Romansh (Swiss). On December 5 in some parts of Switzerland, there is a parade. The people wear huge headdresses shaped like a bishop's hat. The Christmas Child delivers gifts to many Swiss children on Christmas Eve. In French areas, gifts are given on New Year's Day. Bells of all kinds can be heard during the Christmas season. A star is always on top of their Christmas tree.

POLAND

The children of Poland receive gifts twice during the holiday season. The larger gifts arrive on December 6 from St. Nicholas. On Christmas Eve, the Star Man leaves smaller gifts. People wait for the first star to appear on Christmas Eve to begin celebrating. The dinner table is covered with straw. Over the straw is a white tablecloth. This reminds the people of Christ's birth in a stable. Decorations include sheaves of grain and a decorated fir tree. The tree is always decorated with stars, angels, and an ornament that resembles a spider web. Celebrations continue until Star Man's last visit on January 6.

CZECHOSLOVAKIA

In Czechoslovakia, December 6 is called *Svaty Mikalas Day.* Svaty Mikalas slides down a golden cord from heaven to see if the children know their prayers. They rush to the table to recite them. If they do a good job, the angel who comes with Svaty gives them gifts. If not, the devil called *Cert* rattles his chains to scare them!

On December 24, the tree is lighted and gifts are placed underneath. The tree is decorated with gingerbread shapes, colored paper, fabric, and egg ornaments. Nativity scenes are often shaped from bread dough. It is a custom to cut open an apple to predict the future.

UKRAINE

Many of the Ukraine's Christmas customs are in keeping with Czechoslovakia and Russia. However, the country has its own custom of placing a spider web on the Christmas tree for good luck. The legend of the web tells of a poor woman who could not afford to decorate a tree for her children. In the morning, the tree's branches were covered with spider webs which turned to silver as soon as the sun rose.

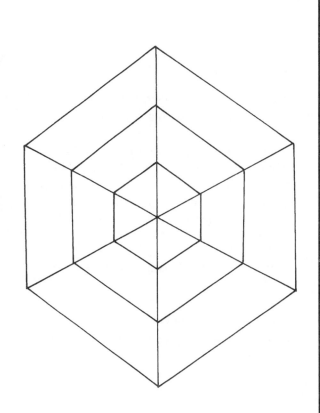

RUSSIA

Hristos Razdajetsja! is the Russian Christmas greeting. There are two gift bearers in Russia: a man dressed in red with a white beard called *Dyed Maroz* (Grandfather Frost) and an old woman named Babouschka. The legend of *Babouschka* is similar to Italy's Befana. She was too busy spinning to go with the Three Kings when they searched for the Christ Child, so now she must wander forever and deliver gifts to good children. She visits on Epiphany. A favorite gift is a nested doll called the *Matryoshka* doll.

PHILIPPINES

The Christmas celebrations in the Philippines start with a bang! On December 16, firecrackers and bamboo cannons blast and bells ring. Then, there is a church service. Christmas Eve and Day include church as well as visits with family and friends. Parties and gift giving continue until Three King's Day, January 6.

The Christmas star is the main symbol of the holiday. Some stars are very large and beautiful, though no star is placed on a Christmas tree because, in the Philippines, it is not customary to have a Christmas tree.

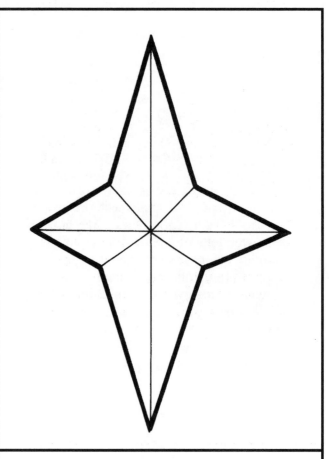

CHINA

Paper lanterns, chains, and flowers are the most popular Chinese Christmas decorations. Sometimes special lanterns are shaped like pagodas. They show the Holy Family inside. Children in China hang up stockings and wait for *Lan Khoong-Khoong* (Nice Old Father) to fill them with small gifts. Santa Claus is also known in China. He is called *Christmas Old Man.*

New Year's Day is a bigger year-end celebration than is Christmas for the Chinese people. This is primarily because there are not many Christians in China.

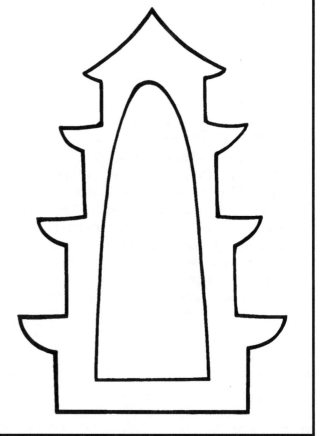

JAPAN

The Japanese Christmas greeting is *Meri Kurisumasu!* There are not many Christians in this country, but Christmas is a time for Christians to host important programs in their churches to share their message with others.

The people here celebrate in some of the same ways as Americans and Canadians. Trees are decorated, but they use paper fans, lanterns, dolls, and flowers. The one who brings gifts is called *Hoteiosho.* He is a Japanese god who has eyes in the back of his head to see everything the children do. However, many Japanese families enjoy Santa's visit, too.

THAILAND

Since most people in Thailand are not Christians, Christmas is not celebrated by many. Those who do celebrate it enjoy caroling and church activities. They have trees decorated with paper garlands and large manger scenes. Ornaments and decorations are made of woven straw. Fish are a common ornament pattern.

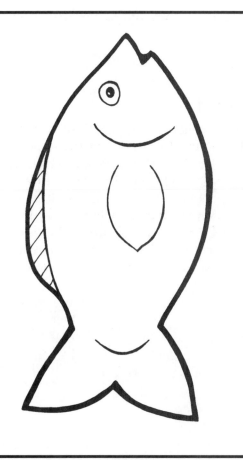

GREECE

A Greek Christmas celebration begins on December 6 with the Feast of St. Nicholas. St. Nicholas does not deliver gifts to children in Greece, but he is an important saint to the seamen. St. Basil delivers gifts to children on January 1. The legend of St. Basil tells of his generosity to poor girls. He is said to have tossed special cakes called *vasilopita* through their windows. These cakes had a coin hidden inside. The coin was especially for their dowries so they might marry. Another legend tells of goblin-type beings who make trouble around Christmas. They disappear on January 6.

There are also special traditions during the Greek Christmas Eve meal. For one, the people lift the table with their hands three times before eating.

BRAZIL

The weather is warm at Christmastime in Brazil. Church services can be held outside. Papa Noël is the gift giver. He enters through an open window to put presents into children's shoes. It is a tradition in Brazil to help the poor by giving white-wrapped gifts at the midnight mass. The gifts contain white foods such as flour, potatoes, and rice. The manger scene in Brazil is called the *presebre*. Children make figures from brightly-colored sawdust. Often there is a tree covered with cotton designed to look like snow. Legend says the animals can speak on Christmas Eve!

MEXICO

The Mexican greeting is *Feliz Navidad!* *Las Posadas* is a very important Mexican custom. It begins on December 16 and lasts until Christmas Eve. Families and friends walk from house to house searching for a place to stay, just like the Holy Family did in Bethlehem. They are always turned away. But at the last home, they are invited in, and there they celebrate with good food and games. Plays called *pastorelas* show the shepherds' journey to Bethlehem. Paper lanterns called *farolitos* light the way for those who search for the Christ Child. Children usually have to wait until January 6 to receive their gifts from the Three Kings. But some children also receive presents from Santa on Christmas Eve.

UNITED STATES AND CANADA

Christmas in Canada and the United States is a busy time of shopping, baking, decorating, and preparing for December 24. The week between Christmas Eve and New Year's is when most parties and celebrations take place. Families generally follow customs from their ancestors.

The gift bearer is Santa Claus. He lives at the North Pole with Mrs. Claus and the elves. They make presents and Santa delivers them in his sleigh pulled by eight reindeer. Santa slides down the chimney and leaves the presents in stockings hung there.

Most homes set up a well-decorated evergreen tree. Brightly colored lights are strung inside, outside, and on the tree. Sending Christmas cards is a popular tradition with many families, too, as is singing carols. Christian families celebrate the holiday with special church services on Christmas Eve and Day.

Patterns

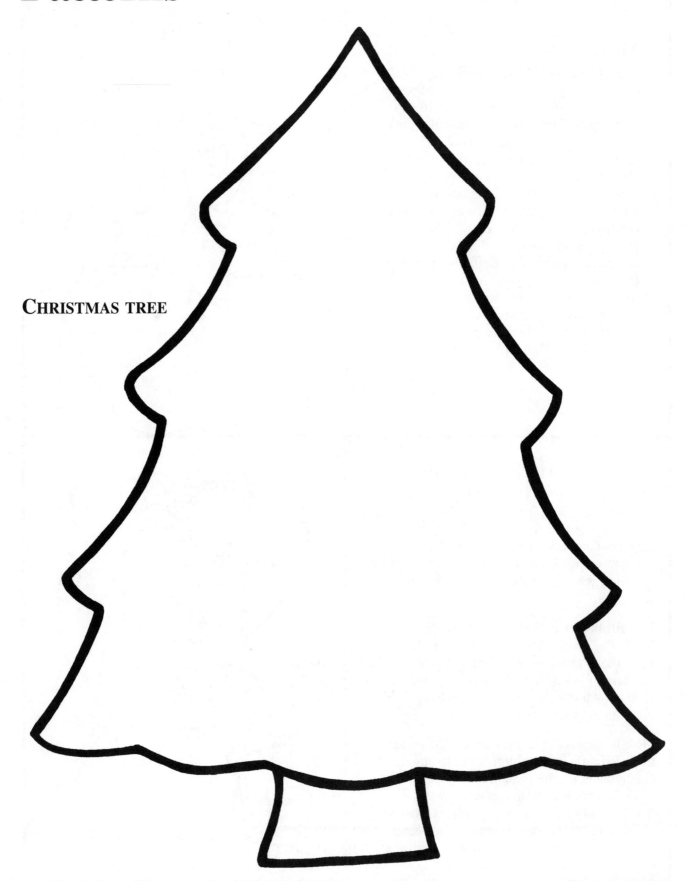

CHRISTMAS TREE

Patterns *(cont.)*

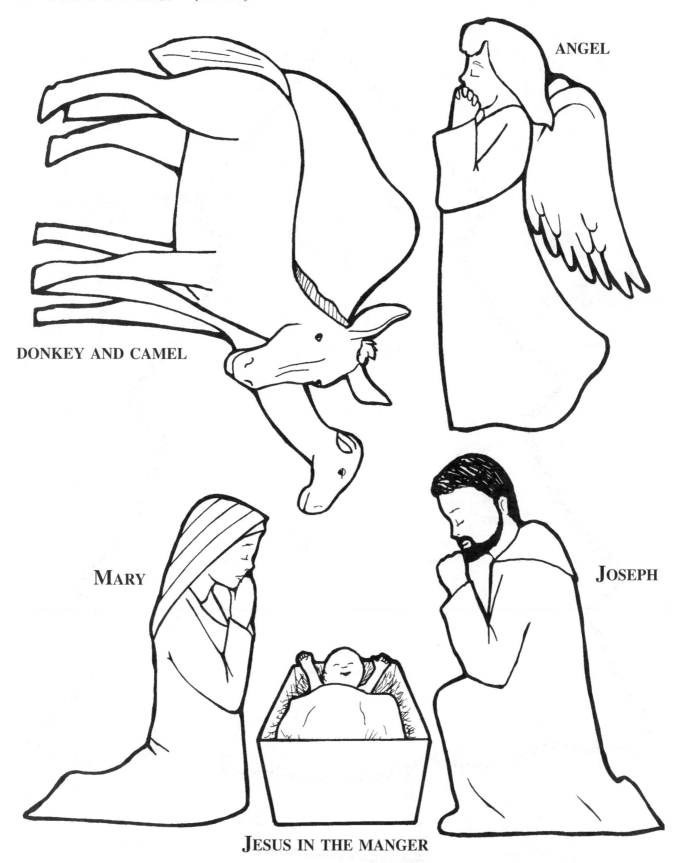

DONKEY AND CAMEL

ANGEL

MARY

JOSEPH

JESUS IN THE MANGER

Patterns *(cont.)*

WISE MEN

SHEPHERD AND SHEEP

Patterns *(cont.)*

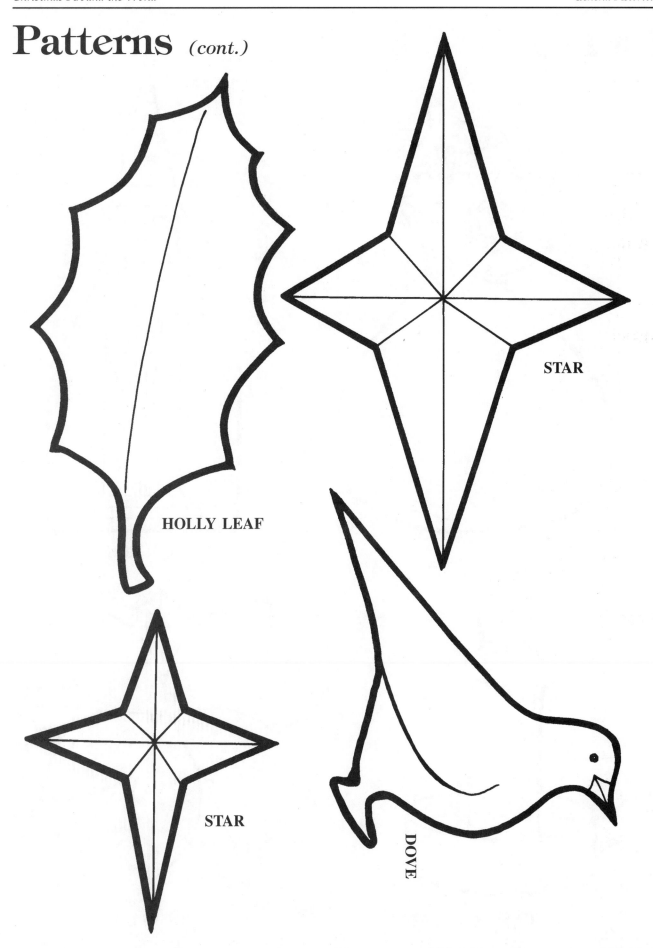

HOLLY LEAF

STAR

STAR

DOVE

Patterns *(cont.)*

TOY BAG

CHURCH

CANDLE

POINSETTIA

Patterns *(cont.)*

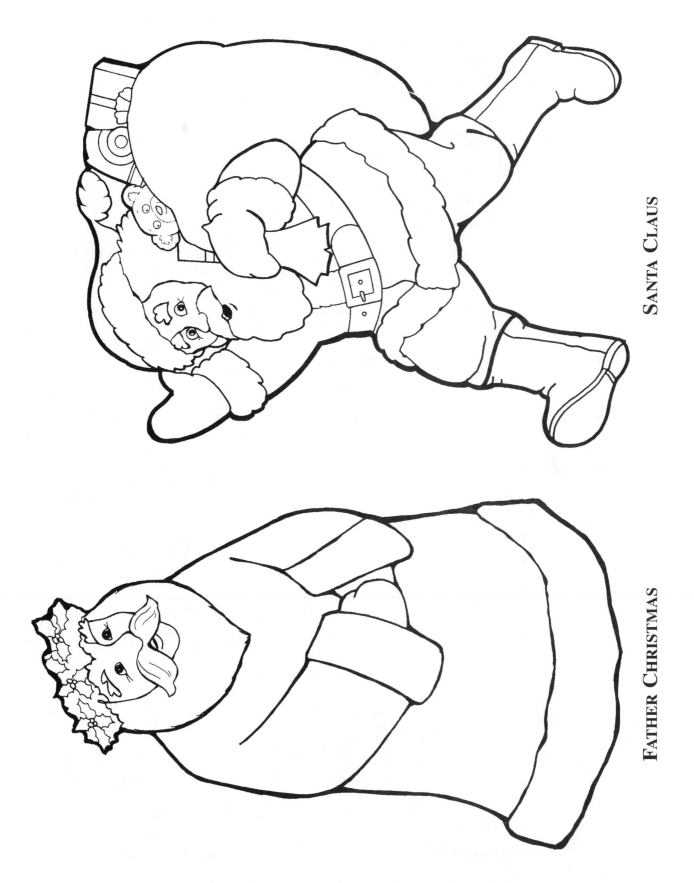

SANTA CLAUS

FATHER CHRISTMAS

Patterns *(cont.)*

GINGERBREAD MAN

Patterns *(cont.)*

BELLS

CANDY CANE

WREATH

NISSE/ELF

Patterns *(cont.)*

REINDEER

TREES

GIFTS

STOCKING

Patterns *(cont.)*

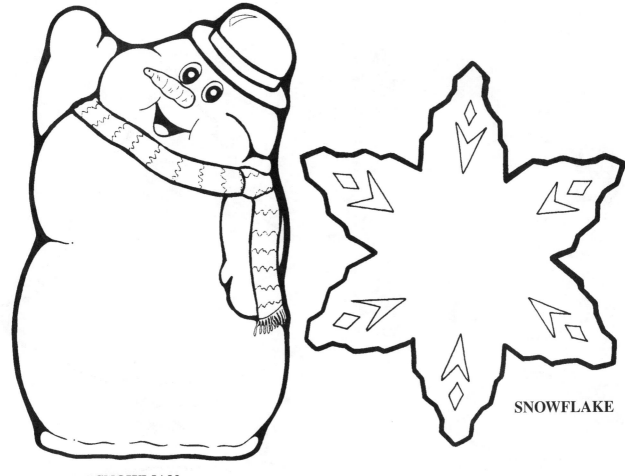

SNOWFLAKE

SNOWMAN

ROSE

ORNAMENT

Patterns *(cont.)*

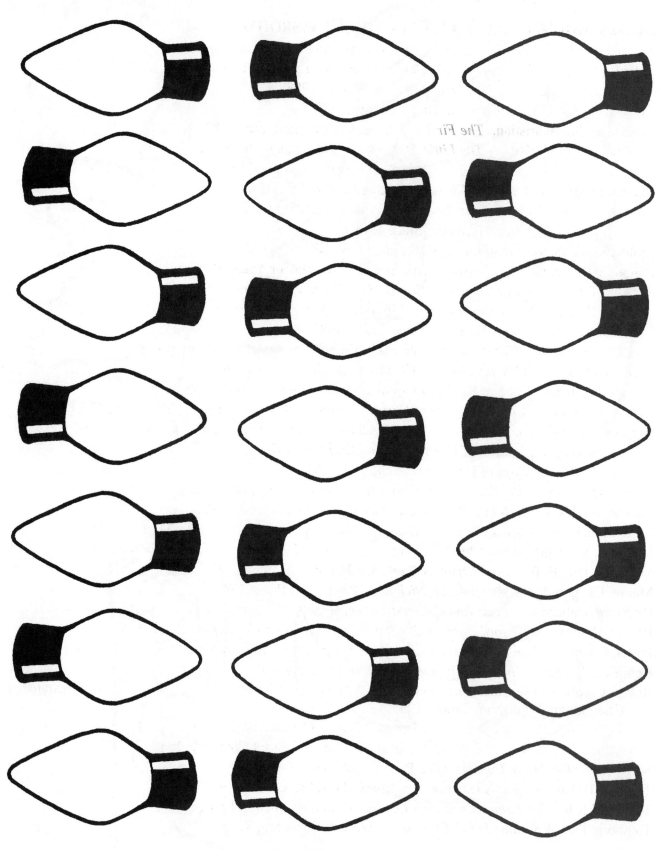

LIGHT BULBS

Bibliography

BOOKS AND STORIES TO USE IN THE CLASSROOM

Adler, Susan S. *Samantha's Surprise: A Christmas Story*. Pleasant Company, 1986.

Ahlberg, Janet and Allan. *The Jolly Christmas Postman*. Little, Brown and Co., 1991.

Alcott, Louisa May. *Little Women*. Alfred A. Knopf, 1988.

Aliki. *Christmas Tree Memories*. HarperCollins, 1991.

Andersen, Hans Christian. *The Fir Tree*. Creative Education, Inc., 1983.

Andersen, Hans Christian. *The Little Match Girl*. The Putnam Publishing Group, 1990.

Arico, Diane. *A Season of Joy: Favorite Stories and Poems for Christmas*. Doubleday & Co., 1987.

Boland, Emily. *An American Christmas*. Allied Books Ltd., 1989.

Brett, Jan. *The Wild Christmas Reindeer*. G.P. Putnam's Sons, 1990.

Bunting, Eve. *Night Tree*. Harcourt Brace Jovanovich, 1991.

Childcraft. *Volume 9: Holidays and Birthdays*. World Book, 1987.

Daniel, Mark. *A Child's Christmas Treasury*. Dial Books for Young Readers, 1991.

dePaola, Tomie. *Book of Christmas Carols*. G.P. Putnam and Sons, 1987.

Dickens, Charles. *A Christmas Carol*. Airmont Publishing Co., 1963.

Gibbons, Gail. *Christmas Time*. Holiday House, 1982.

Grahame, Kenneth. "Christmas at Mole End" (in *Wind in the Willows*). H. Holt & Co., 1986.

Green, Donna. *We Wish You a Merry Christmas*. Gallery Books, 1990.

Grimm, Jacob and Wilhelm K. *The Elves and the Shoemaker*. Troll Associates, 1981.

Henderson, Kathy. *A New True Book: Christmas Trees*. Children's Press, 1989.

Higgins, Susan Olson. *The Elves' Christmas Book*. Pumpkin Press Publishing House, 1986.

Jackson, Kathryn. *The Joys of Christmas*. Golden Press, 1976.

Kent, Jack. *Twelve Days of Christmas*. Scholastic, 1973.

Low, Alice. *The Family Read-Aloud Christmas Treasury*. Little Brown and Co., 1991.

McRae, Patrick T. *A Child's Book of Christmas*. Children's Press, 1988.

Miller, Edna. *Mousekin's Christmas Eve*. Treehouse Paperbacks, 1972.

Milne, A.A. "King John's Christmas" (in *Now We Are Six*). Dutton Children's Books, 1988.

Moncure, Jane Belk. *Our Christmas Book*. Child's World, 1986.

Moore, Clement C. *A Visit from St. Nicholas*. Peter Piper Press, 1985.

Paterson, Katherine. *Angels and Other Strangers: Family Christmas Stories*. Thomas Crowell, 1979.

Pepper, Dennis. *An Oxford Book of Christmas Stories*. Oxford University Press, 1988.

Porter, Connie. *Addie's Surprise: A Christmas Story*. Pleasant Company, 1994.

Robinson, Barbara. *The Best Christmas Pageant Ever*. Avon Books, 1972.

Royds, Caroline. *The Christmas Book: Stories, Poems, and Carols for the Twelve Days of Christmas*. The Putnam Publishing Group, 1985.

Seuss, Dr. *How the Grinch Stole Christmas!* Random House, 1957.

Shaw, Janet B. *Kirsten's Surprise: A Christmas Story*. Pleasant Company, 1986.

Soto, Gary. *Too Many Tamales*. The Putnam Publishing Group, 1993.

Thomas, Dylan. *A Child's Christmas in Wales*. David R. Godine, 1980.

Tolkien, J.R.R. *The Father Christmas Letters*. Houghton Mifflin, 1991.

Tornborg, Pat. *A Sesame Street Christmas*. Western Publishing Co., 1982.

Bibliography *(cont.)*

BOOKS AND STORIES TO USE IN THE CLASSROOM *(cont.)*

Törnqvist, Rita. *The Christmas Carp.* R&S Books, 1990.

Tripp, Valerie. *Felicity's Surprise: A Christmas Story.* Pleasant Company, 1991.

Tripp, Valerie. *Molly's Surprise: A Christmas Story.* Pleasant Company, 1986.

Van Allsburg, Chris. *The Polar Express.* Houghton Mifflin, 1985.

Wilder, Laura Ingalls. *Farmer Boy.* Harper & Row, 1971.

Wilder, Laura Ingalls. *Little House in the Big Woods.* Harper & Row, 1971.

Wilder, Laura Ingalls. *Little House on the Prairie.* Harper & Row, 1971.

RESOURCE BOOKS

Barth, Edna. *Holly, Reindeer, and Colored Lights: The Story of Christmas Symbols.* Clarion, 1971.

Chalmers, Irena. *The Great American Christmas Almanac.* Viking Penguin, 1988.

Cohen, Hennig, and Tristram Potter Coffin. *The Folklore of American Holidays.* Gale Research Company, 1987.

Duden, Jane. *Christmas.* Macmillan, 1990.

Ebel, Holly. *Christmas in the Air.* HollyDay Books, 1986.

Egan, Louise Betts. *The Whole Christmas Catalogue for Kids.* Price Stern Sloan, 1988.

Foley, Daniel J. *Christmas the World Over.* Chilton Books, 1963.

Fowler, Virginia. *Christmas Crafts and Customs Around the World.* Prentice-Hall, 1984.

Gober, Lasley F. *The Christmas Lover's Handbook.* Betterway Publications, 1985.

Graube, Iretta Sitts. *Thematic Unit: Christmas.* Teacher Created Resources, 1992.

Hautzig, Esther. *Christmas Goodies.* Random House, 1981.

Jasmine, Julia. *Multicultural Holidays.* Teacher Created Resources, 1994.

Jones, E. Willis. *The Santa Claus Book.* Walker and Company, 1978.

Joseph, Robert. *The Christmas Book.* McAfee Books, 1978.

Karas, Sheryl. *The Solstice Evergreen.* Aslan Publishing, 1991.

Kurelek, William. *A Northern Nativity.* Tundra Books, 1976.

Milninaire, Catherine. *Celebrations.* Harmony Books, 1981.

Oliver, Jane. *The Doubleday Christmas Treasury.* Doubleday & Co., 1986.

Werneke, Herbert H. *Celebrating Christmas Around the World.* The Westminster Press, 1962.

Wezeman, Phyllis Vos and Jude Dennis Fournier. *Joy to the World.* Ave Maria Press, 1992.

MUSIC

Bach. *Christmas Oratorio.* Allegro, 1984.

Handel. *The Messiah.* Academy of Ancient Music, 1980.

Tchaikovsky. *The Nutcracker Suite.* London Records, 1973.

Answer Key

Page 100: Christmas Wordsearch

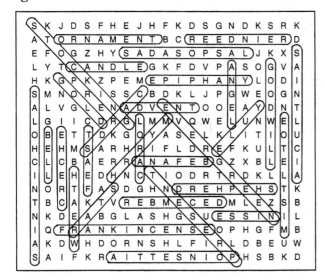

Page 101: Who Are the Gift Bearers?

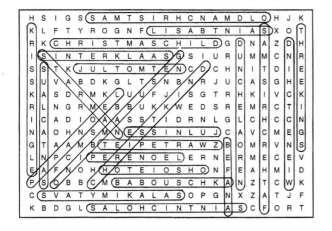

Page 105: Christmas Codes

Santa Claus is coming to town.

Page 107: Math Code Munchies

gingerbread

A = 3
B = 6
C = 9
D = 12
E = 18
F = 21
G = 24
H = 28
I = 30
J = 32
K = 34
L = 36
M = 38
N = 40
O = 15
P = 27
Q = 35
R = 2
S = 4
T = 14
U = 16
V = 20
W = 42
X = 45
Y = 48
Z = 49

Answer Key *(cont.)*

Page 108: Gift-Wrapped Map

614 x 6 = 3,684
3,684 ÷ 12 = 307
307 - 169 = 138
138 x 25 = 3,450
3,450 - 1897 = 1,553
1,554 + 2579 = 4,132
4,132 ÷ 4 = 1,033
1,033 + 597 = 1,630
1,630 x 20% = 326
326 x 1/2 = 163
163 - 138 = 25
Total = 25

Page 110: Where Are We?

1. The smallest state is Rhode Island. The largest state is Alaska. Individual routes will vary.
2. The Atlantic Ocean is between Norway and Newfoundland.
3. The children in Philadelphia are probably up. It is 10 A.M.
4. Answers will vary.
5. Many early U.S. and Canadian immigrants came from European countries. They brought their traditions with them.
6. The gift bearer will spend the most time in Mexico City because Mexico City has the largest population in the world.

Page 112: Searching for Christmas

Christmas, Florida 32709

Mistletoe, Kentucky 41351

Rudolph, Ohio 43462

Santa Claus, Indiana 47579

Snowflake, Virginia 24251

Noel, Missouri 64854

North Pole, New York 12946; North Pole, Colorado 80901

Star, Texas 76880; Star, Idaho 83669; Star, Mississippi 39167; Star, North Carolina 27356

Star City, Arkansas 71667; Star City, West Virginia 26505

Antler, North Dakota 58711

Holiday, Florida 34690

Carol City, Florida 33055

Note: Perhaps your students wish to write a letter to Santa in a classroom writing exercise. You can write the response letter and have it sent back to them from one of the above towns.

Index

Activities and Crafts

Activities

*Page 111 mentions specific information concerning each of the following countries: Australia, Columbia, Ghana, India, Korea, Liberia, Puerto Rico, Syria, and Turkey.)

**In addition to these activities, most country sections suggest stories and language arts activities related to the culture.

Crafts

Index (cont.)

Index *(cont.)*

Carols

Gift Bearers and Their Helpers

Index (cont.)